AIRCAM AVIATION SERIES

Mk. I, No. 1 RCAF Squadron (later No. 401 RCAF Squadron), Croydon, August 1940. P3080.
Under surface: Sky   Code: Dark Sea Grey

BATTLE OF BRITAIN
HAWKER HURRICANE SUPERMARINE SPITFIRE
MESSERSCHMITT Bf.109

Illustrated by Richard Ward
Compiled by Peter G. Cooksley & Richard Ward
Text by Christopher F. Shores

THE VIRGIN

Personal insignia in white on camouflage.

Mk. Ia, No. 616 'South Yorkshire' Squadron, flown by Flt. Lt. D. E. Gillam. N3093.
Sky under surfaces with black port wing.

PUBLISHED BY
OSPREY PUBLICATIONS LTD., ENGLAND.

EDITORIAL OFFICE:
P.O. BOX No. 5,
CANTERBURY, KENT, ENGLAND.

© Osprey Publications Ltd. SBN 85045 006 3
THE BERKSHIRE PRINTING CO. LTD., READING, ENGLAND

SUBSCRIPTION & BUSINESS OFFICE:
P.O. BOX 25, 707 OXFORD ROAD,
READING, BERKSHIRE, ENGLAND.

FIRST PUBLISHED 1969
SECOND IMPRESSION 1970
THIRD IMPRESSION 1971

THE HURRICANE AND SPITFIRE

The two main single-engined, single-seat fighter aircraft of the Royal Air Force in 1940, the Hawker Hurricane and the Supermarine Spitfire, gained considerable fame and an assured place in history for their part in the Battle of Britain. The Spitfire was undoubtedly the more advanced design of the pair, more pleasing to the eye and offering both a higher performance and a greater sensitivity of control than the Hurricane. However, it was not available in anything like the same numbers as the Hawker machine, which, although bearing the brunt of the Battle, was overshadowed in the public eye by its more glamorous stable-mate. A similar situation existed among the pilots of these machines, few people nowadays realising that the majority of the pilots engaged in the Battle were N.C.O.s, and the much more widely publicised officers were in fact in the minority.

At the start of July 1940, when the initial phase of the Battle began with German attacks on shipping in the English Channel, both aircraft had already been tested in combat over France, the Hurricane throughout the fighting on the Continent, the Spitfire during the Dunkirk evacuation, and both had shown up well. In July the air defence of Great Britain, in the hands of Fighter Command, was the responsibility of three operational Groups, No. 11 covering the south of England, including London, No. 12 covering the Midlands, and No. 13 covering the north of England, Scotland and Northern Ireland. These three Groups had under their command 44 squadrons of single-seat fighters, 19 of these flying Spitfires, and 25 Hurricanes. Twenty-three were within 11 Group, 15 with Hurricanes, and many of those within other Groups were scarcely more than cadre units, reassembling and re-equipping after the withdrawal from France, or newly-forming.

By early August, when the Luftwaffe launched the first full-scale attacks against the English mainland, striking at radar stations and fighter airfields, the strength of Fighter Command had risen to 47 squadrons, and a new Group, No. 10, had been formed to relieve 11 Group of the responsibility of defending south-west England. This new Group disposed 7 squadrons, increased a month later to 8, and by the end of September to 9, 11 Group being reduced by 4 squadrons.

August was the worst month for the British fighters, attacks on fighter airfields and on the early warning system seriously reducing the number of pilots available, and by late August the Command had a deficit of over 200 pilots to the establishment. Fortunately Hitler's instructions that the attack of the Luftwaffe should be shifted to London saved Fighter Command, and during September new Hurricane units began arriving, the first Canadian, Polish and Czech squadrons going into action.

Throughout the Battle squadrons were frequently rotated between Groups, to allow those which had been heavily engaged to rest and recoup. Unfortunately, some squadrons which were ordered to the south were decimated in their early actions, and the more successful units were thrown back into the fighting almost at once. Certain squadrons in the north, particularly those recovering from the French campaign, served more as operational training units, so many of their pilots being posted to bring other squadrons up to strength as soon as they were fully trained, that these squadrons were never able to enter the Battle in their own right. By the end of September, when the German daylight bomber attacks virtually ceased and the remainder of the Battle became a series of fights at high altitude between fighter and fighter-bomber formations, Fighter Command had reached a strength of 51 squadrons, 32 of Hurricanes, but still only 19 of Spitfires.

Early in the Battle it had become obvious that the Hurricane was out-performed by the German Messerschmitt Bf 109E in all but manoeuvreability, whereas the Spitfire was the latter's equal. Consequently, whenever possible a squadron of Spitfires and one of Hurricanes operated together, the former to engage the escorting fighters, the latter to attack the bombers. To this task the Hurricane was ideally suited, being a first-rate firing platform, and capable of sustaining considerable damage from return fire. Mark II versions of both the Hurricane and Spitfire arrived with the squadrons late in the Battle, both offering increased maximum speed and better altitude performance, but despite this, the Battle was fought mainly by the Mark I versions of both aircraft. Both powered by the same Rolls Royce Merlin engine, and carrying similar armament of 8 wing-mounted .303 in. Browning machine guns (although cannon-armed examples of both aircraft were operationally tested during the Battle), performance was:—

	Maximum Speed	Service Ceiling
Hawker Hurricane I	325 m.p.h.	34,000 ft.
Hawker Hurricane IIa	342 m.p.h.	35,000 ft.
Supermarine Spitfire I	355 m.p.h.	34,000 ft.
Supermarine Spitfire IIa	370 m.p.h.	35,000 ft.

By the end of the Battle in early November, two more Groups had been formed, No. 9 with 2 squadrons for the defence of the west Midlands, and No. 14, also with 2 squadrons, for the defence of north Scotland. Strength was 53 squadrons and 2 flights, but 21 of these, including all in 9, 13 and 14 Groups and most in 12 Group, had been designated 'C' class squadrons — not operational, but training pilots for the front line units, while 2 more were 'B' class — operational in emergency only. A further 3 Hurricane squadrons and one flight had been ordered to train as night-fighter units. Pilot strength at this stage had increased to a point where it exceeded establishment by nearly 70.

Squadrons operating during the Battle of Britain, July - October 1940, were:—

Hurricanes: 1, 3, 17, 32, 43, 46, 56, 73, 79, 85, 87, 111, 145, 151, 213, 229, 232, 238, 242, 245, 249, 253, 257, 263, 302 (Polish), 303 (Polish), 310 (Czech), 312 (Czech), 501, 504, 601, 605, 607, 615, 1 R.C.A.F., 422 Flight.

Spitfires: 19, 41, 54, 64, 65, 66, 72, 74, 92, 152, 222, 234, 266, 602, 603, 609, 610, 611, 616, 421 Flight.

SPECIFICATIONS

HAWKER HURRICANE Mk. I
Rolls-Royce Merlin III, 1,030 h.p.

Armament	8 × 0.303 Browning M.G's in wings.	Height	13 ft. 1½ in.
		Wing Area	258 sq. ft.
		Wt. Loaded	6,447 lb.
		Max. Speed	328 m.p.h.
Span	40 ft. 0 in.	Max. Range	505 miles
Length	31 ft. 6 in.	Ser. Ceiling	34,200 ft.

SUPERMARINE SPITFIRE Mk. Ia
Rolls-Royce Merlin III, 1,030 h.p.

Armament	8 × 0.303 Browning M.G's in wings.	Height	12 ft. 3 in.
		Wing Area	242 sq. ft.
		Wt. Loaded	6,200 lb.
		Max. Speed	367 m.p.h.
Span	36 ft. 10 in.	Max. Range	400 miles
Length	29 ft. 11 in.	Ser. Ceiling	31,900 ft.

MESSERSCHMITT Bf.109E
Daimler-Benz DB 601A, 1,150 h.p.

Armament	2 × 7.9 mm. MG 17 M.G's on top of fuselage firing through airscrew disc. 2 × 20 mm. MG FF cannon in wings.	Span	32 ft. 4½ in.
		Length	28 ft. 8 in.
		Height	11 ft. 2 in.
		Wing Area	174 sq. ft.
		Wt. Loaded	5,520 lb.
		Max. Speed	357 m.p.h.
		Max. Range	412 miles
		Ser. Ceiling	36,000 ft.

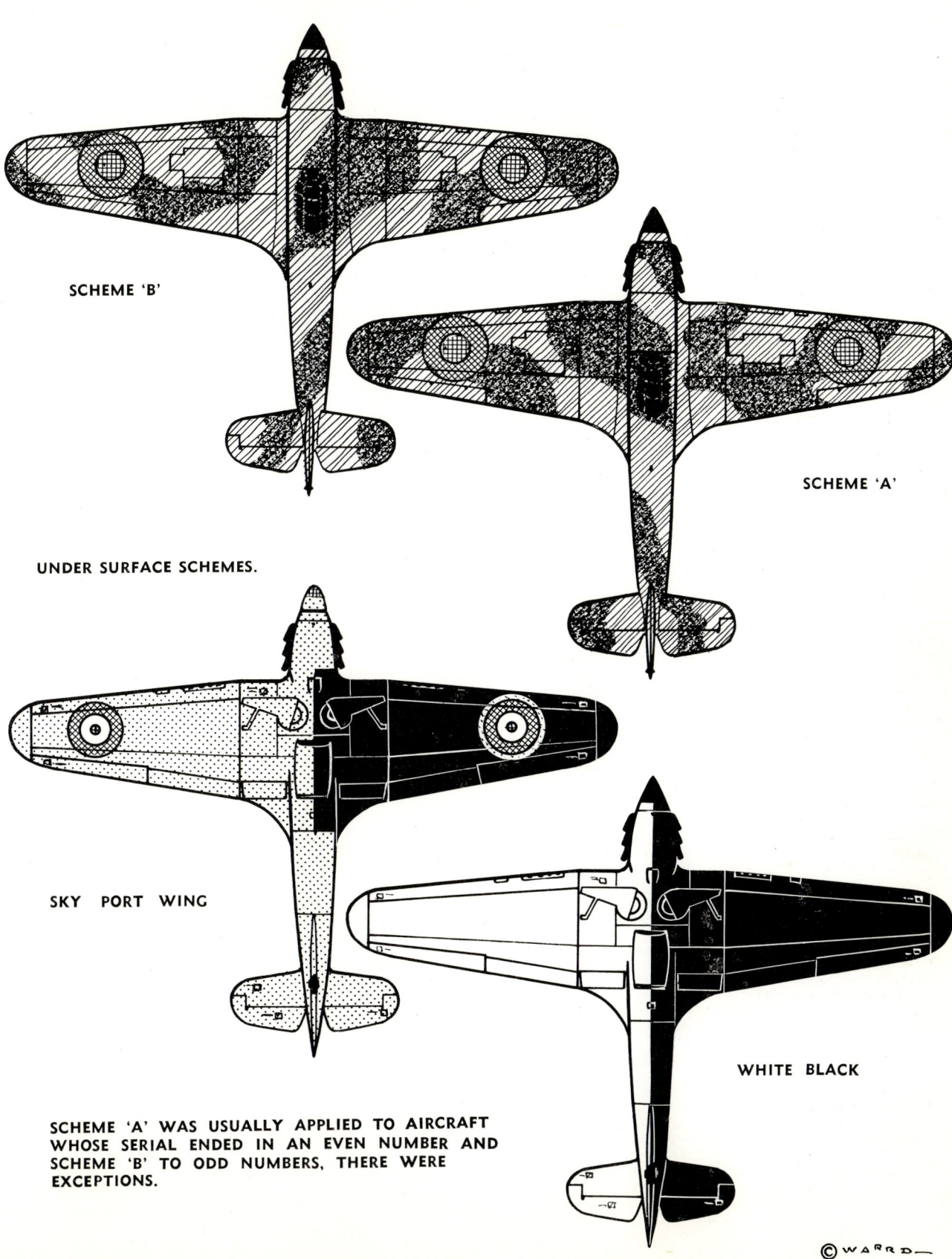

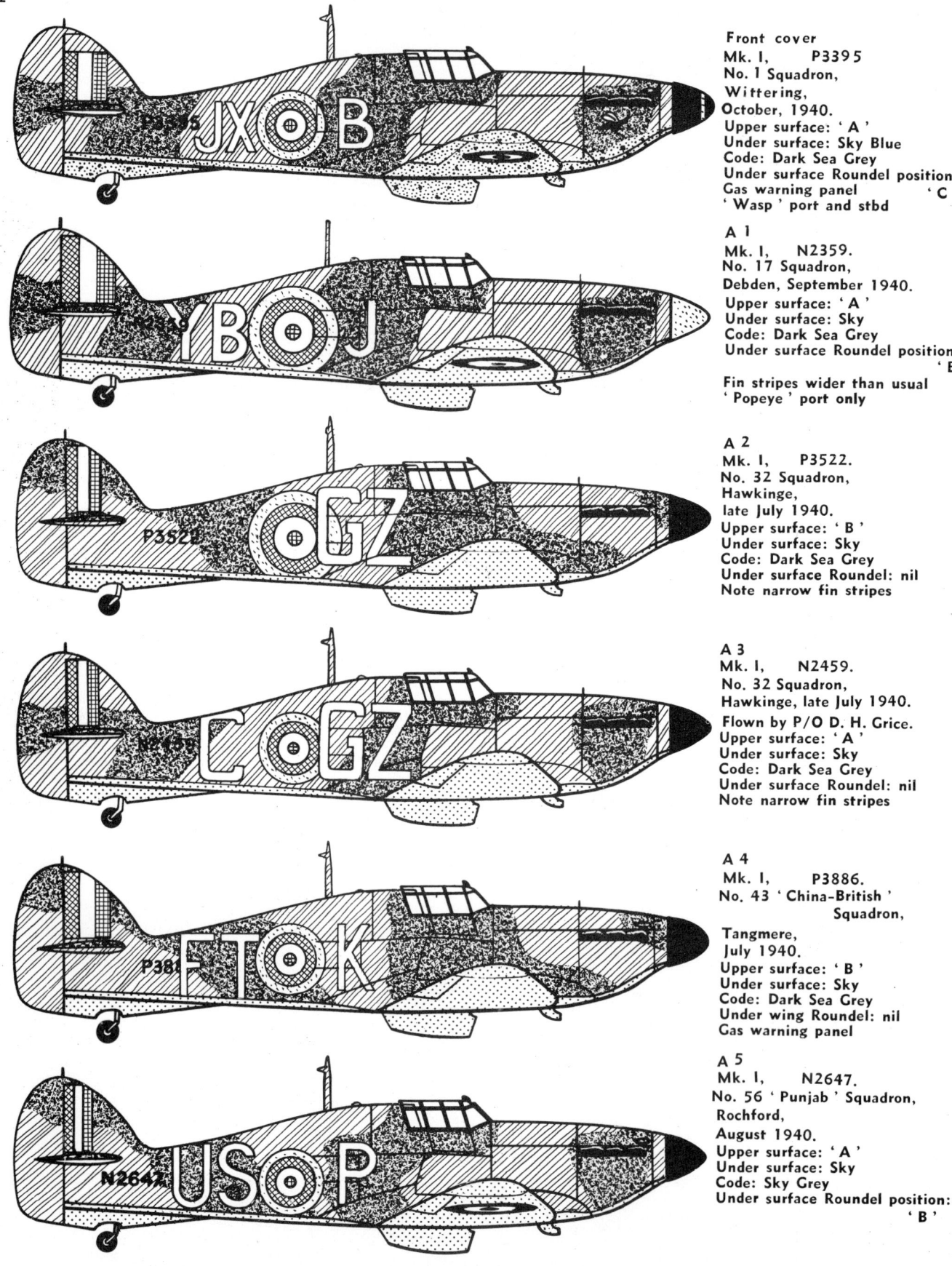

Front cover
Mk. I,   P3395
No. 1 Squadron,
Wittering,
October, 1940.
Upper surface: 'A'
Under surface: Sky Blue
Code: Dark Sea Grey
Under surface Roundel position:
Gas warning panel   'C'
'Wasp' port and stbd

A 1
Mk. I,   N2359.
No. 17 Squadron,
Debden, September 1940.
Upper surface: 'A'
Under surface: Sky
Code: Dark Sea Grey
Under surface Roundel position:
                                        'B'
Fin stripes wider than usual
'Popeye' port only

A 2
Mk. I,   P3522.
No. 32 Squadron,
Hawkinge,
late July 1940.
Upper surface: 'B'
Under surface: Sky
Code: Dark Sea Grey
Under surface Roundel: nil
Note narrow fin stripes

A 3
Mk. I,   N2459.
No. 32 Squadron,
Hawkinge, late July 1940.
Flown by P/O D. H. Grice.
Upper surface: 'A'
Under surface: Sky
Code: Dark Sea Grey
Under surface Roundel: nil
Note narrow fin stripes

A 4
Mk. I,   P3886.
No. 43 'China-British'
                 Squadron,
Tangmere,
July 1940.
Upper surface: 'B'
Under surface: Sky
Code: Dark Sea Grey
Under wing Roundel: nil
Gas warning panel

A 5
Mk. I,   N2647.
No. 56 'Punjab' Squadron,
Rochford,
August 1940.
Upper surface: 'A'
Under surface: Sky
Code: Sky Grey
Under surface Roundel position:
                                        'B'

A 6
Mk. I, P3854.
No. 85 Squadron,
Church Fenton,
September 1940.
Upper surface: 'B'
Under surface: Sky
Code: Dark Sea Grey
Under surface Roundel
    position: 'A'
Note exhaust glare shield
Hexagon port only

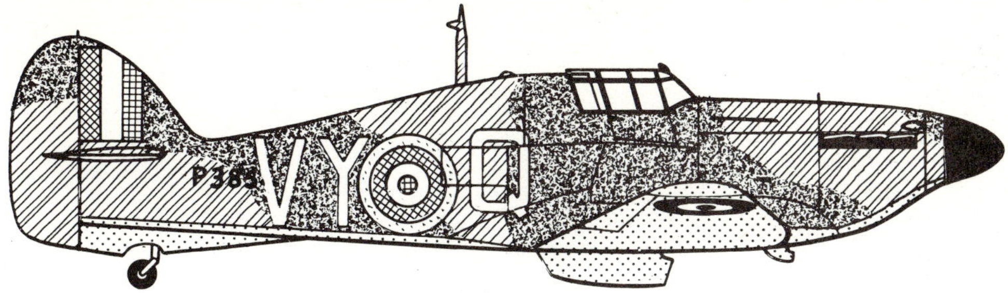

B 1
Mk. I, V6611.
No. 85 Squadron,
Church Fenton,
September 1940.
Upper surface: 'A'
Under surface: Sky Blue
Code: Dark Sea Grey
Under surface Roundel
    position: 'C'
Hexagon port only

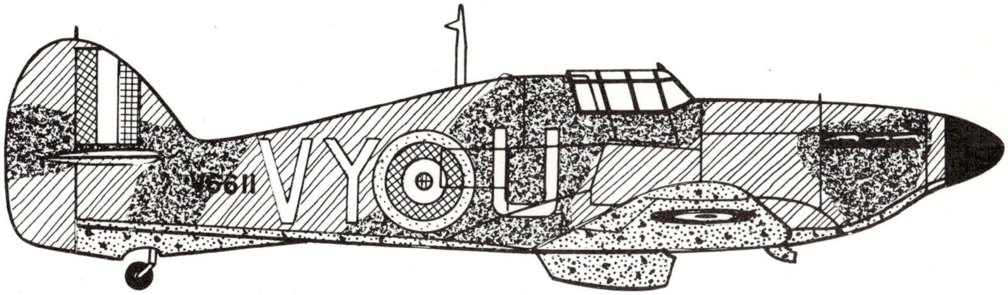

B 2
Mk. I, P2798.
No. 87 'United Provinces'
    Squadron,
Exeter, August 1940.
Flown by
    Flt. Lt. I. R. Gleed.
Upper surface: 'B'
Under surface: Azure Blue
Code: Dark Sea Grey
Under surface Roundel
    position: 'C'
Personal insignia stbd. side only

B 3
Mk. I, P3880.
No. 111 Squadron,
Croydon, June 1940.
Upper surface: 'B'
Under surface: Sky
Code: Sea Grey
Under surface Roundel
    position: 'C'

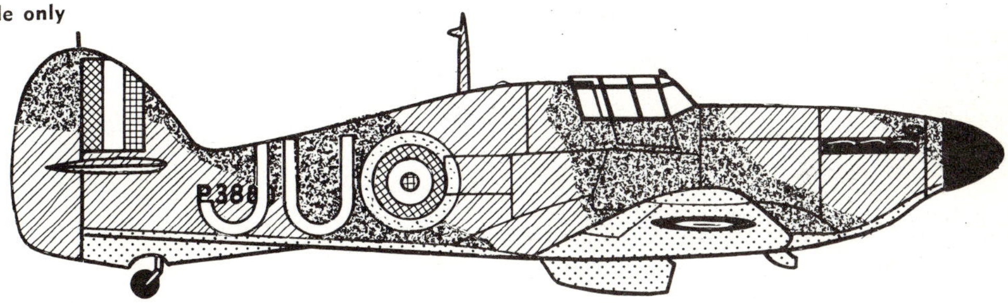

B 4
Mk. I, N3822.
No. 145 Squadron,
West Hampnett,
July 1940.
Upper surface: 'B'
Under surface:
Black/White down CL
Code: Sky Grey
Under surface Roundel
    position: 'B'

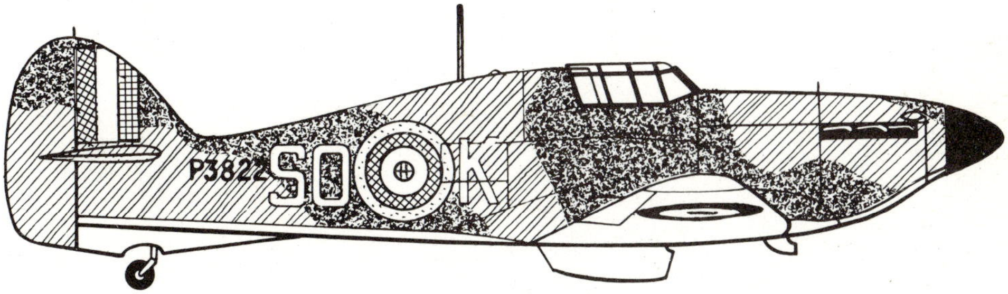

B 5
Mk. I, P3320.
No. 151 Squadron,
North Weald,
late August 1940.
Upper surface: 'B'
Under surface: Sky
Code: Sea Grey
Under surface Roundel
    position: 'C'

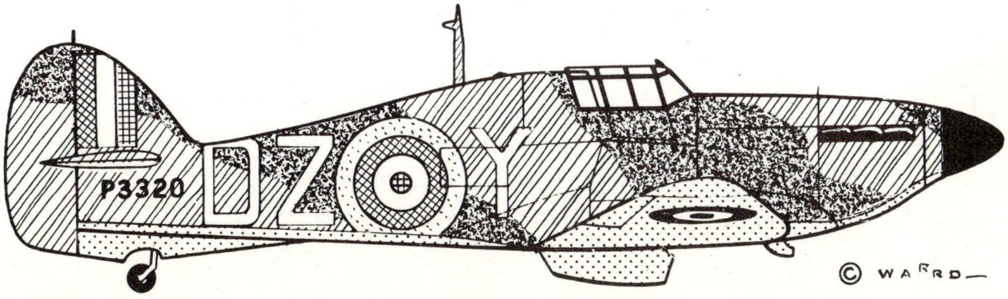

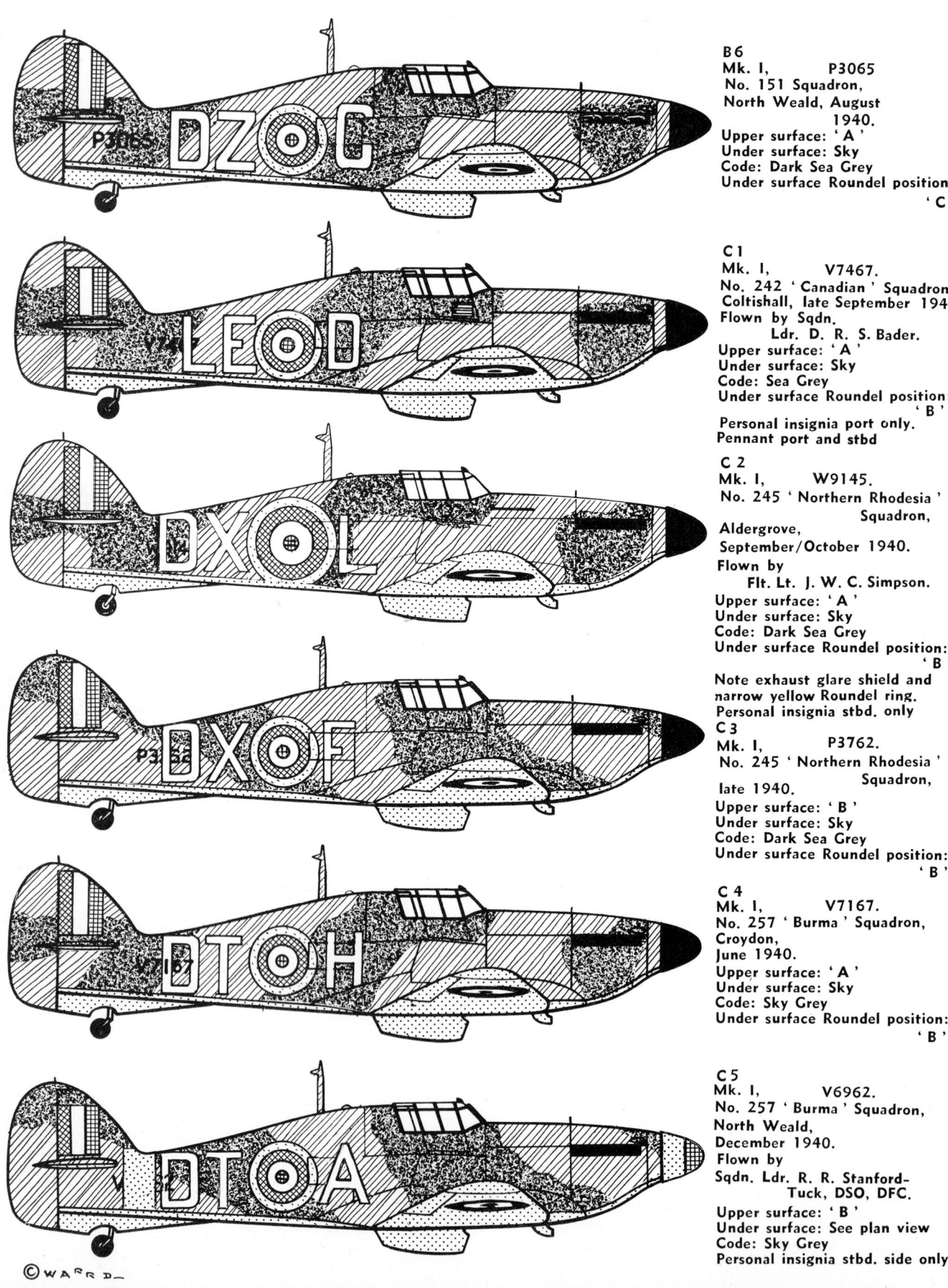

B 6
Mk. I, P3065
No. 151 Squadron,
North Weald, August 1940.
Upper surface: 'A'
Under surface: Sky
Code: Dark Sea Grey
Under surface Roundel position: 'C'

C 1
Mk. I, V7467.
No. 242 'Canadian' Squadron,
Coltishall, late September 1940.
Flown by Sqdn.
  Ldr. D. R. S. Bader.
Upper surface: 'A'
Under surface: Sky
Code: Sea Grey
Under surface Roundel position: 'B'
Personal insignia port only.
Pennant port and stbd

C 2
Mk. I, W9145.
No. 245 'Northern Rhodesia' Squadron,
Aldergrove,
September/October 1940.
Flown by
  Flt. Lt. J. W. C. Simpson.
Upper surface: 'A'
Under surface: Sky
Code: Dark Sea Grey
Under surface Roundel position: 'B'
Note exhaust glare shield and narrow yellow Roundel ring.
Personal insignia stbd. only

C 3
Mk. I, P3762.
No. 245 'Northern Rhodesia' Squadron,
late 1940.
Upper surface: 'B'
Under surface: Sky
Code: Dark Sea Grey
Under surface Roundel position: 'B'

C 4
Mk. I, V7167.
No. 257 'Burma' Squadron,
Croydon,
June 1940.
Upper surface: 'A'
Under surface: Sky
Code: Sky Grey
Under surface Roundel position: 'B'

C 5
Mk. I, V6962.
No. 257 'Burma' Squadron,
North Weald,
December 1940.
Flown by
  Sqdn. Ldr. R. R. Stanford-
    Tuck, DSO, DFC.
Upper surface: 'B'
Under surface: See plan view
Code: Sky Grey
Personal insignia stbd. side only

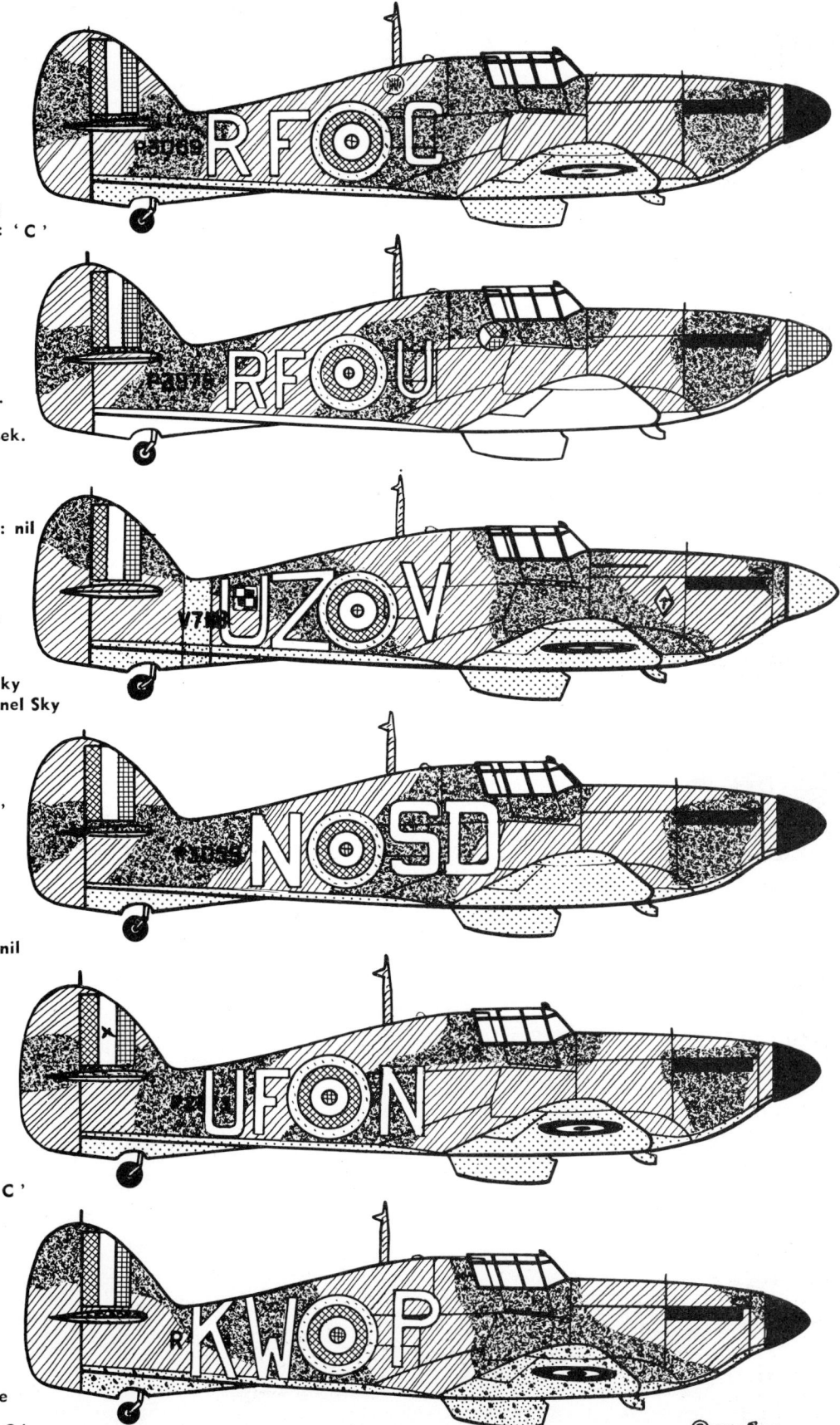

C 6
Mk. I, P3069.
No. 303 ' Kosciusko '
  (Polish) Squadron,
Northolt,
early September 1940.
Upper surface: ' A '
Under surface: Sky
Code: Dark Sea Grey
Under surface Roundel
        position: ' C '
Personal insignia port
    and stbd

D 1
Mk. I, P3975.
No. 303 ' Kosciusko '
  (Polish) Squadron,
Northolt,
early September 1940.
Flown by Sgt. Josef
            Frantisek.
Upper surface: ' A '
Under surface:
Black/White down CL
Code: Dark Sea Grey
Under surface Roundel: nil

D 2
Mk. I, V7118.
No. 306 ' Torun '
  (Polish) Squadron,
Northolt,
December 1940.
Upper surface: ' B '
Under surface: Black/Sky
    down CL, nose panel Sky
Code: Dark Sea Grey

D 3
Mk. I, P3059.
No. 501
' County of Gloucester '
        Squadron,
Gravesend,
mid August 1940.
Upper surface: ' A '
Under surface: Sky
Code: Dark Sea Grey
Under wing Roundels: nil

D 4
Mk. I, P2673.
No. 601
' County of London '
        Squadron,
Tangmere,
August 1940.
Upper surface: ' A '
Under surface: Sky
Code: Dark Sea Grey
Under wing Roundel: ' C '

D 5
Mk. I, R4194.
No. 615
' County of Surrey '
        Squadron,
July/August 1940.
Upper surface: ' B '
Under surface: Sky Blue
Code: Dark Sea Grey
Under wing Roundel: ' C '

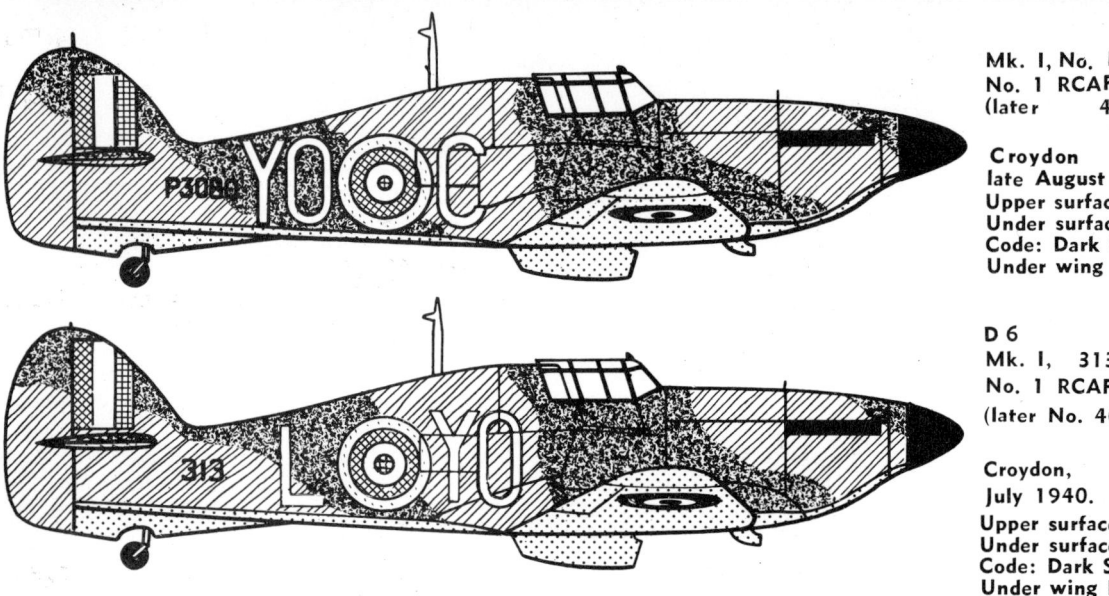

Mk. I, No. P3080.
No. 1 RCAF Squadron,
(later 401 RCAF
Squadron)
Croydon
late August 1940.
Upper surface: 'B'
Under surface: Sky
Code: Dark Sea Grey
Under wing Roundel: 'C'

D 6
Mk. I, 313 (ex L1761).
No. 1 RCAF Squadron
(later No. 401 RCAF
Squadron),
Croydon,
July 1940.
Upper surface: 'B'
Under surface: Sky
Code: Dark Sea Grey
Under wing Roundel: 'C'

Note.
No tint has been applied to the code and aircraft letter on the black and white Hurricane and Spitfire starboard side views, the correct colour will be found in the black and white caption relating to each aircraft. Suffix letters 'A', 'B' and 'C', and in the case of the Spitfire only 'Bi', relate to the roundel position on the under surface of the wing and should not be confused as roundel types. On some black and white side views of the Bf.109E the aircraft number and Gruppe insignia have been illustrated in black, the correct colour will be found on the colour illustrations and in the captions relating to the black and white side views. The shield of JG2 was always silver with the R in red.
Other schemes are known to have existed on Bf.109E's during the Battle of Britain period, for example many aircraft flew in overall dark green, but to date no details for a complete scheme have come to hand.

HURRICANE ROUNDEL POSITIONS AND DIMENSIONS.

STANDARD POSITION OF UPPER SURFACE ROUNDEL

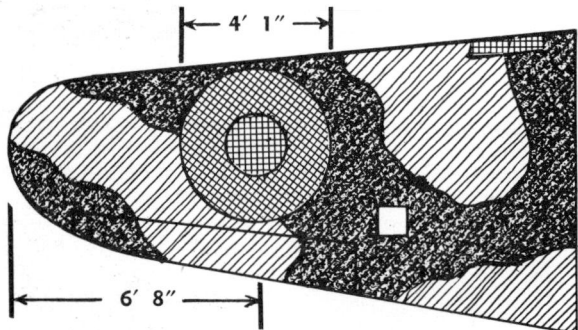

GAS WARNING PANEL APPROX 18" SQUARE.
PORT SIDE ONLY. 9' 6" APPROX TO CL

UNDER SURFACE ROUNDEL POSITION 'B'

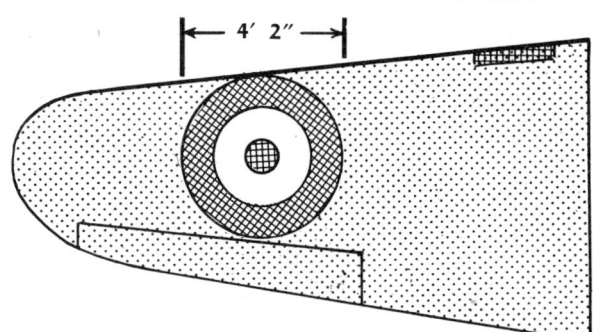

GUN PORT PATCHES WERE USUALLY DOPED RED.

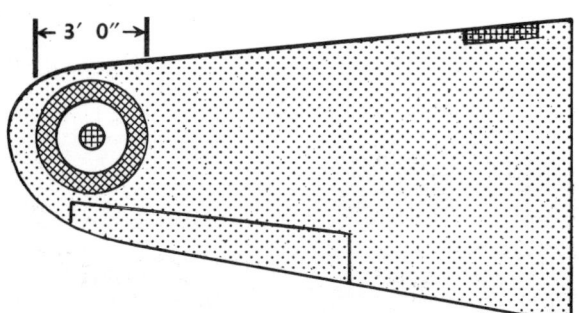

UNDER SURFACE ROUNDEL POSITION 'A'

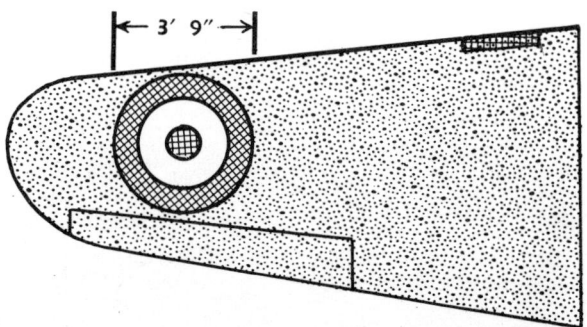

UNDER SURFACE ROUNDEL POSITION 'C'

AIRCAM AVIATION SERIES

UI.S/No. 1

UNIT & PERSONAL INSIGNIA
ROYAL AIR FORCE

Battle of Britain
July 1st - December 31st, 1940

Personal insignia. P/S.
F.O. A. V. Clowes, DFM, No. 1 Squadron.

Personal insignia, No. 17 Squadron. P.

Personal insignia, P.
Flt. Lt. A. L. Deere, No. 54 Squadron.

Presentation insignia, (in yellow). S
YT-D, No. 65 'East India' Squadron.

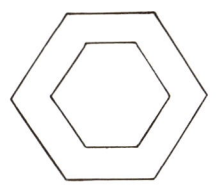
No. 85 Squadron, A Flight. P.

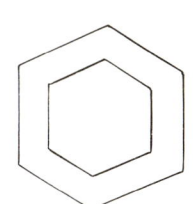
No. 85 Squadron, B Flight. P.

Personal insignia S
Sqdn. Ldr. I. R. Gleed, DFC, 'Figaro',
No. 87 'United Provinces' Squadron.

Personal insignia P.
Sqdn. Ldr. D. R. S. Bader, DSO,
OC No. 242 'Canadian' Squadron.

Personal insignia S.
Sqdn. Ldr. J. W. C. Simpson, DFC.
No. 245 'Northern Rhodesia' Squadron.

To a total of 26. P.
Personal insignia S.
Sqdn. Ldr. R. R. Stanford-Tuck, DSO, DFC,
OC No. 257 'Burma' Squadron.

No. 303 'Kosciuszko' and P/S.
No. 306 'Torun' (Polish) Squadrons.

Personal insignia P/S.
Sgt. Josef Franticek,
No. 303 'Kosciuszko' (Polish) Squadron.

P/S.
No. 303 'Kosciuszko' (Polish) Squadron.

P/S.
No. 306 'Torun' (Polish) Squadron.

P/S.
No. 601 'County of London' Squadron.

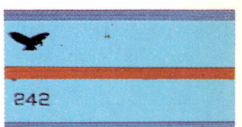
P/S.
Squadron Leaders Pennant as displayed by
Sqdn. Ldr. D. R. S. Bader on V7467.

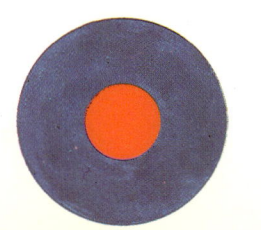
B Type Roundel,
wing upper surfaces. Common to all aircraft.

A1 Type Roundel, fuselage.

A(ii) Type Roundel, wing under surfaces.

A(ii) Type Roundel,
with thin yellow surround on black under surface.

A

1
Mk. I, No. 17 Squadron, Debden, September 1940. N2359.

2
Mk. I, No 32 Squadron, Hawkinge, late July 1940. P3522.

3
Mk. I, No. 32 Squadron, Hawkinge, late July 1940. N2459. Flown by P/O D. H. Grice.

4
Mk. I, No. 43 'China-British' Squadron, Tangmere, July 1940. P3886.

5
Mk. I, No. 56 'Punjab' Squadron, Rochford, August 1940. N2647.

6
Mk. I, No. 85 Squadron, Church Fenton, September 1940. P3854.

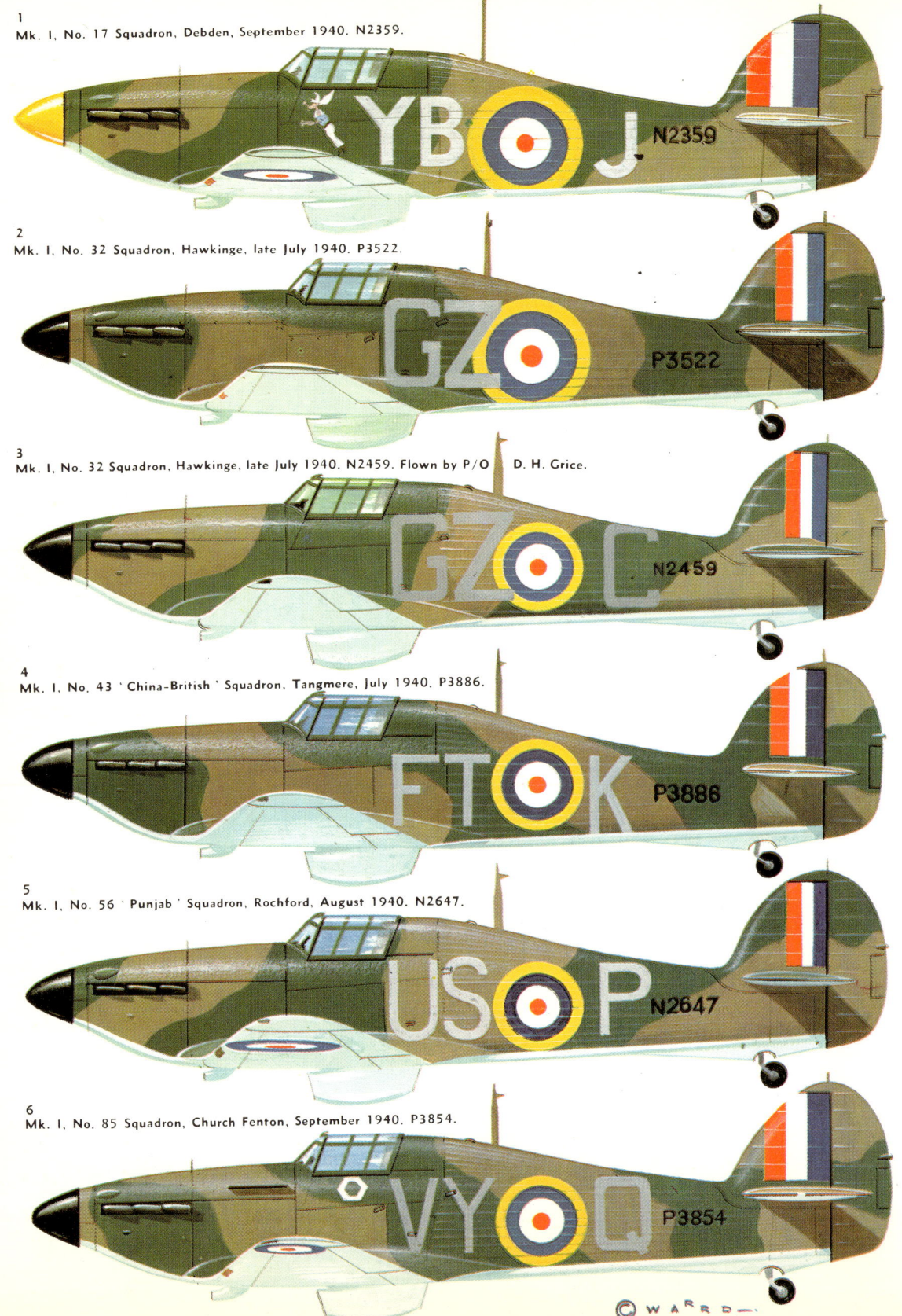

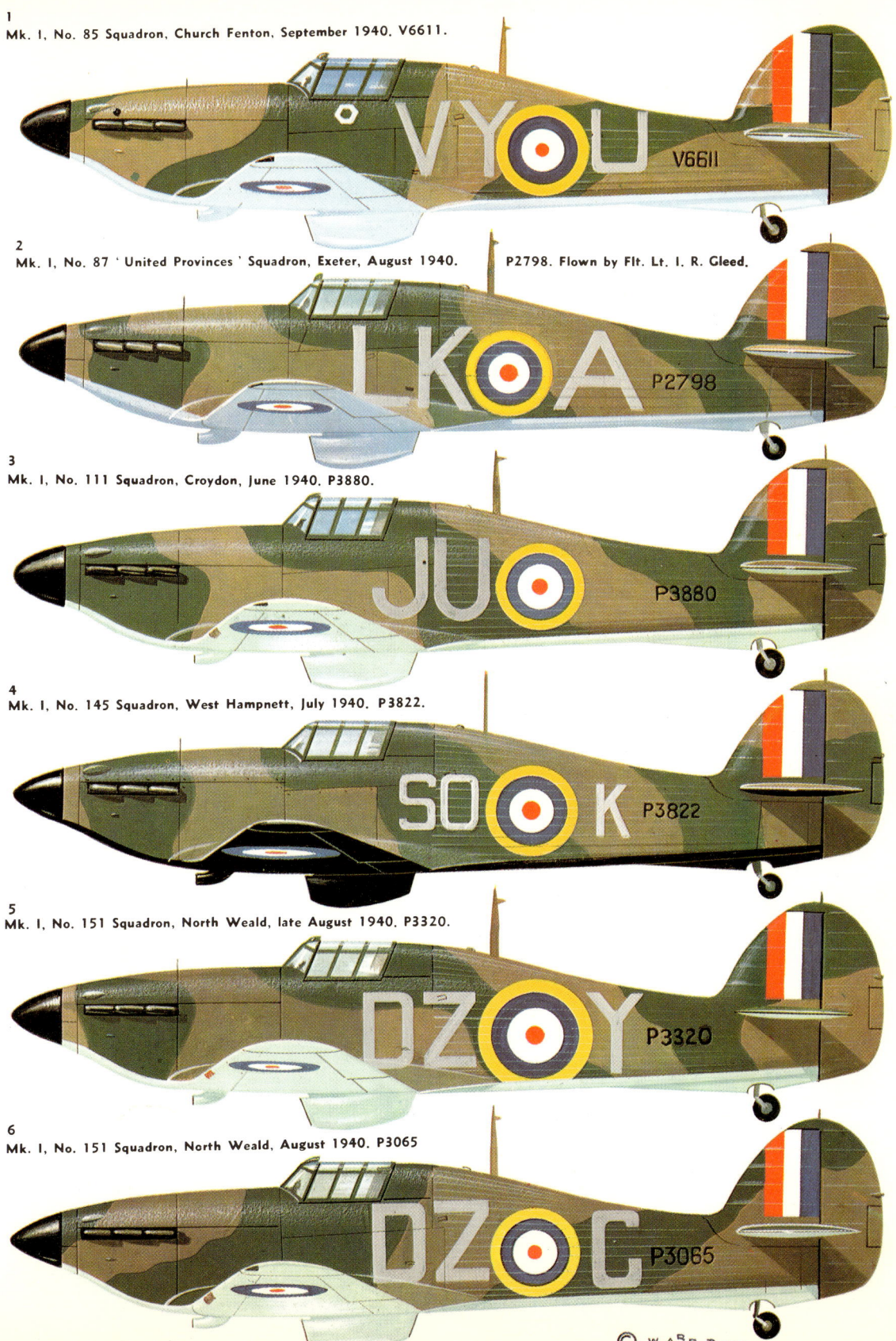

1
Mk. I, No. 85 Squadron, Church Fenton, September 1940. V6611.

2
Mk. I, No. 87 'United Provinces' Squadron, Exeter, August 1940. P2798. Flown by Flt. Lt. I. R. Gleed.

3
Mk. I, No. 111 Squadron, Croydon, June 1940. P3880.

4
Mk. I, No. 145 Squadron, West Hampnett, July 1940. P3822.

5
Mk. I, No. 151 Squadron, North Weald, late August 1940. P3320.

6
Mk. I, No. 151 Squadron, North Weald, August 1940. P3065

C

1
Mk. I, No. 242 'Canadian' Squadron, Coltishall, late September 1940. V7467. Flown by Sqdn. Ldr. D. R. S. Bader.

2
Mk. I, No. 245 'Northern Rhodesia' Squadron, Aldergrove, September/October 1940. W9145. Flown by Flt. Lt. J. W. C. Simpson.

3
Mk. I, No. 245 'Northern Rhodesia' Squadron, late 1940. P3762.

4
Mk. I, No. 257 'Burma' Squadron, Croydon, June 1940. V7167.

5
Mk. I, No. 257 'Burma' Squadron, North Weald, December 1940. V6962. Flown by Sqdn. Ldr. R. R. Stanford-Tuck, DSO, DFC.

6
Mk. I, No. 303 'Kosciusko' (Polish) Squadron, Northolt, early September 1940. P3069.

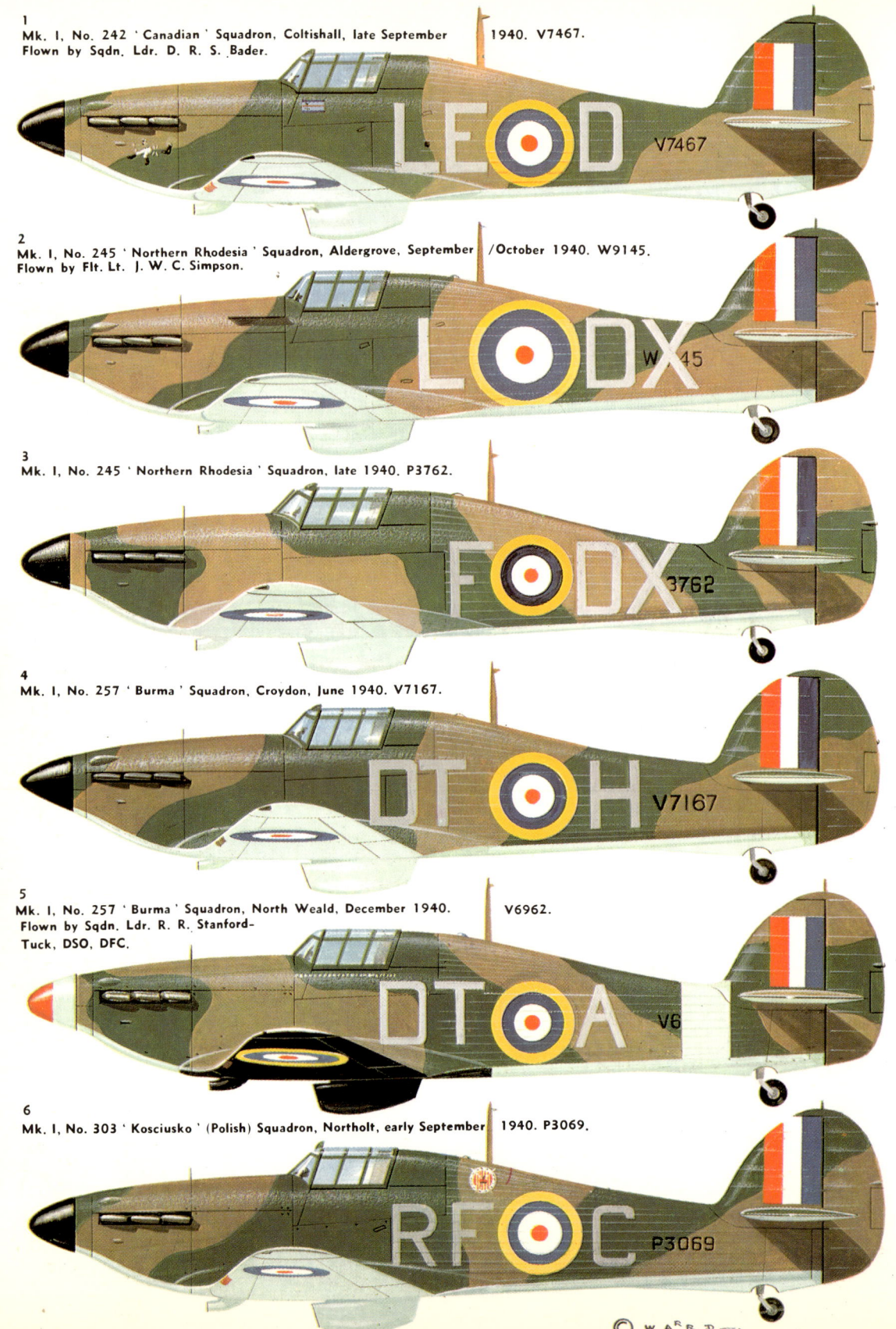

D

1 Mk. I, No. 303 'Kosciusko' (Polish) Squadron, Northolt, early September 1940. P3975. Flown by Sgt. Josef Frantisek.

2 Mk. I, No. 306 'Torun' (Polish) Squadron, Northolt, December 1940. V7118.

5 Mk. I, No. 501 'County of Gloucester' Squadron, Gravesend, mid August 1940. P3059. Flown by P/O K. N. T. Lee.

4 Mk. I, No. 601 'County of London' Squadron, Tangmere, August 1940. P2673.

3 Mk. I, No. 615 'County of Surrey' Squadron, July/August 1940. R4194.

6 Mk. I, No. 1 RCAF Squadron (later No. 401 RCAF Squadron), Croydon, July 1940. 313 (ex L1761).

E

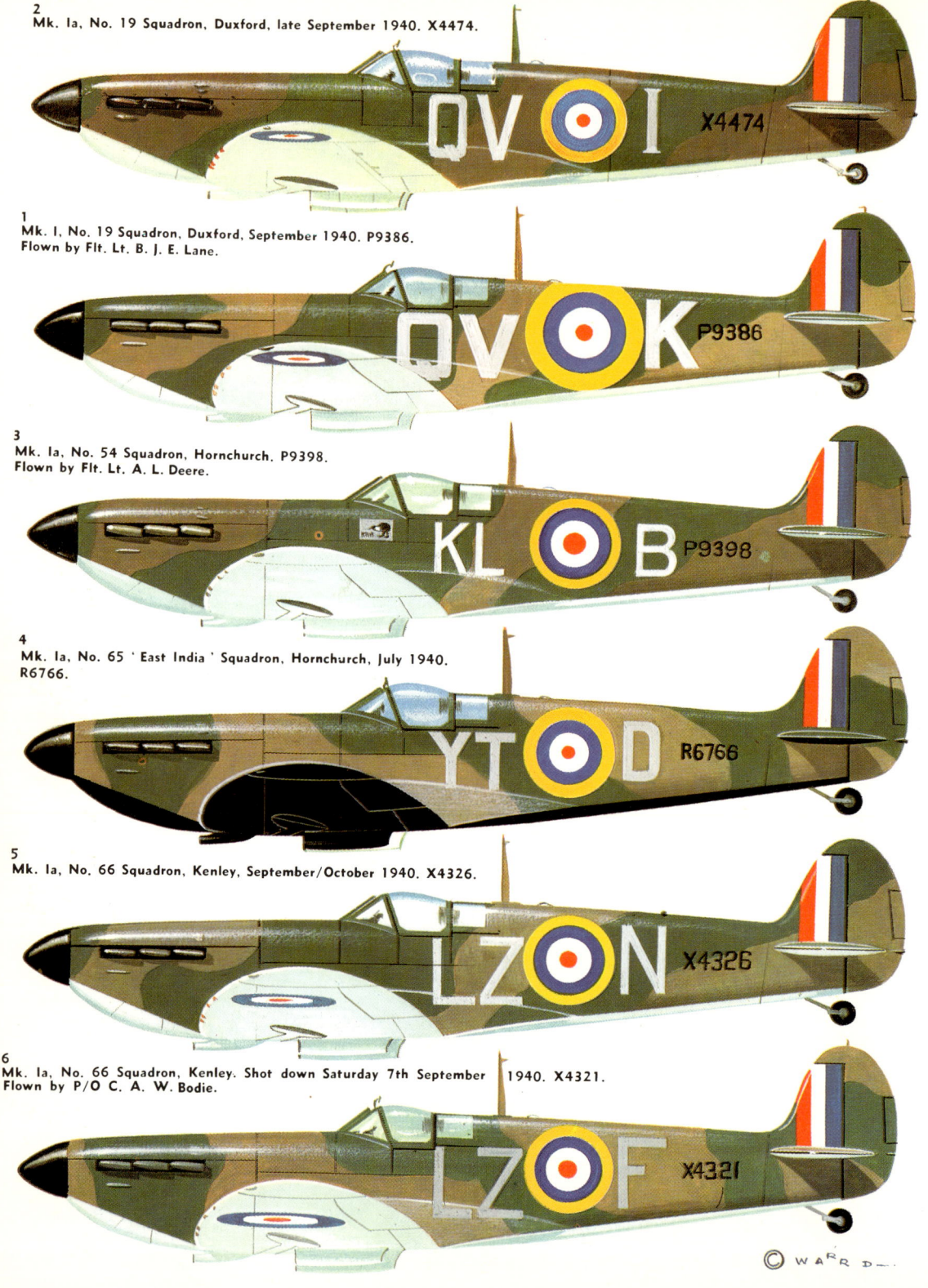

2
Mk. Ia, No. 19 Squadron, Duxford, late September 1940. X4474.

1
Mk. I, No. 19 Squadron, Duxford, September 1940. P9386.
Flown by Flt. Lt. B. J. E. Lane.

3
Mk. Ia, No. 54 Squadron, Hornchurch. P9398.
Flown by Flt. Lt. A. L. Deere.

4
Mk. Ia, No. 65 'East India' Squadron, Hornchurch, July 1940.
R6766.

5
Mk. Ia, No. 66 Squadron, Kenley, September/October 1940. X4326.

6
Mk. Ia, No. 66 Squadron, Kenley. Shot down Saturday 7th September 1940. X4321.
Flown by P/O C. A. W. Bodie.

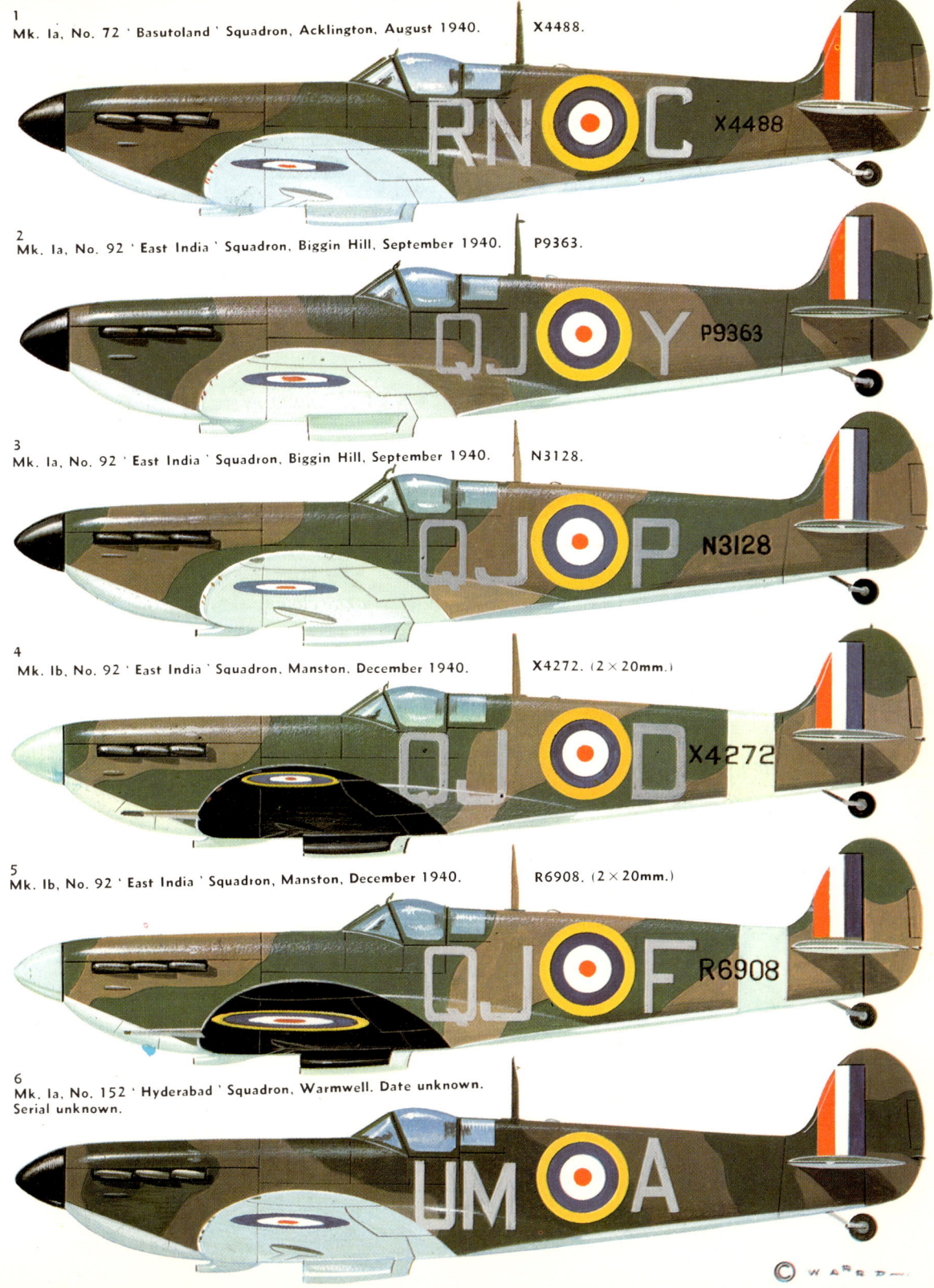

1 Mk. Ia, No. 72 'Basutoland' Squadron, Acklington, August 1940.   X4488.

2 Mk. Ia, No. 92 'East India' Squadron, Biggin Hill, September 1940.   P9363.

3 Mk. Ia, No. 92 'East India' Squadron, Biggin Hill, September 1940.   N3128.

4 Mk. Ib, No. 92 'East India' Squadron, Manston, December 1940.   X4272. (2 × 20mm.)

5 Mk. Ib, No. 92 'East India' Squadron, Manston, December 1940.   R6908. (2 × 20mm.)

6 Mk. Ia, No. 152 'Hyderabad' Squadron, Warmwell. Date unknown. Serial unknown.

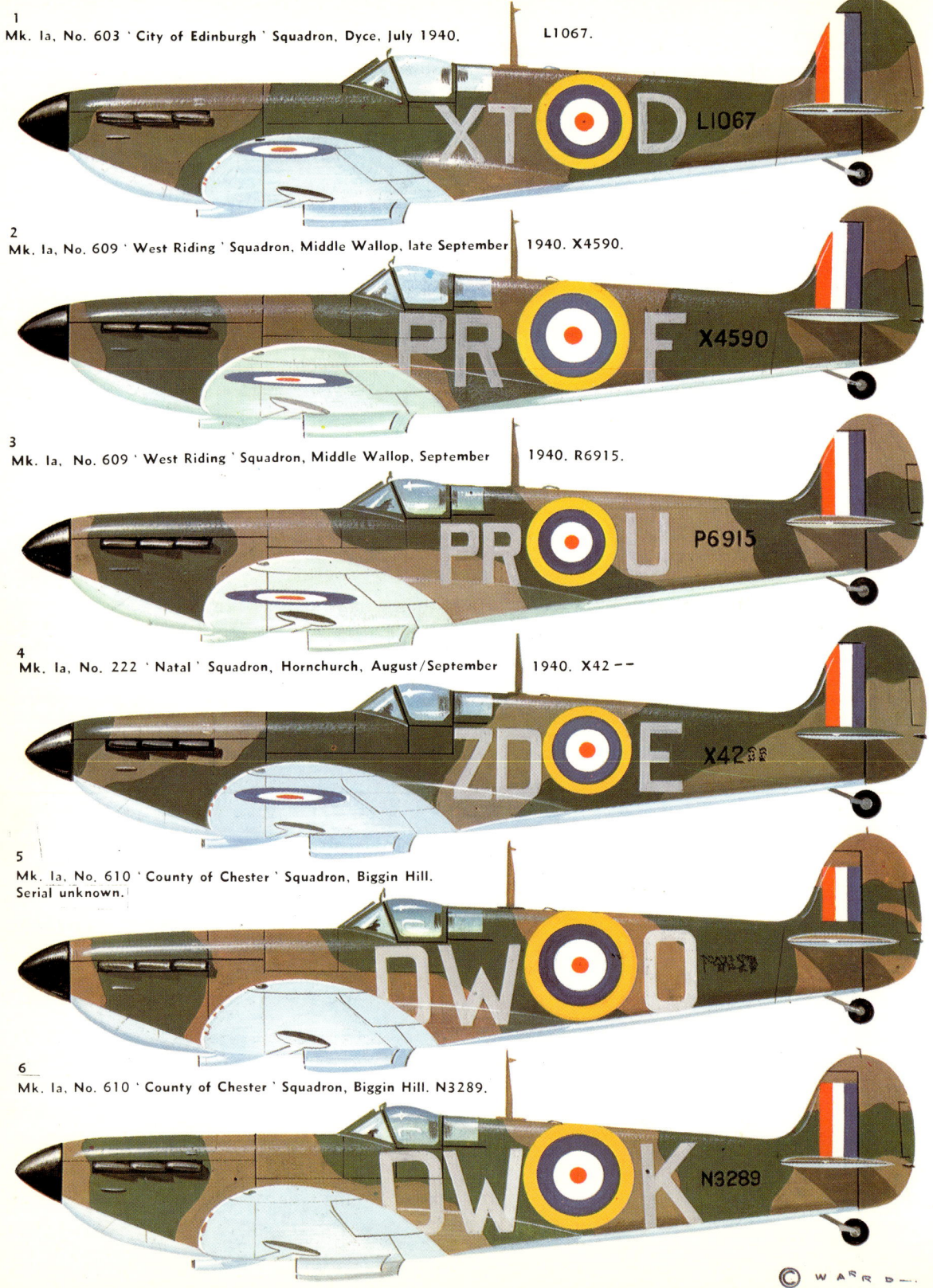

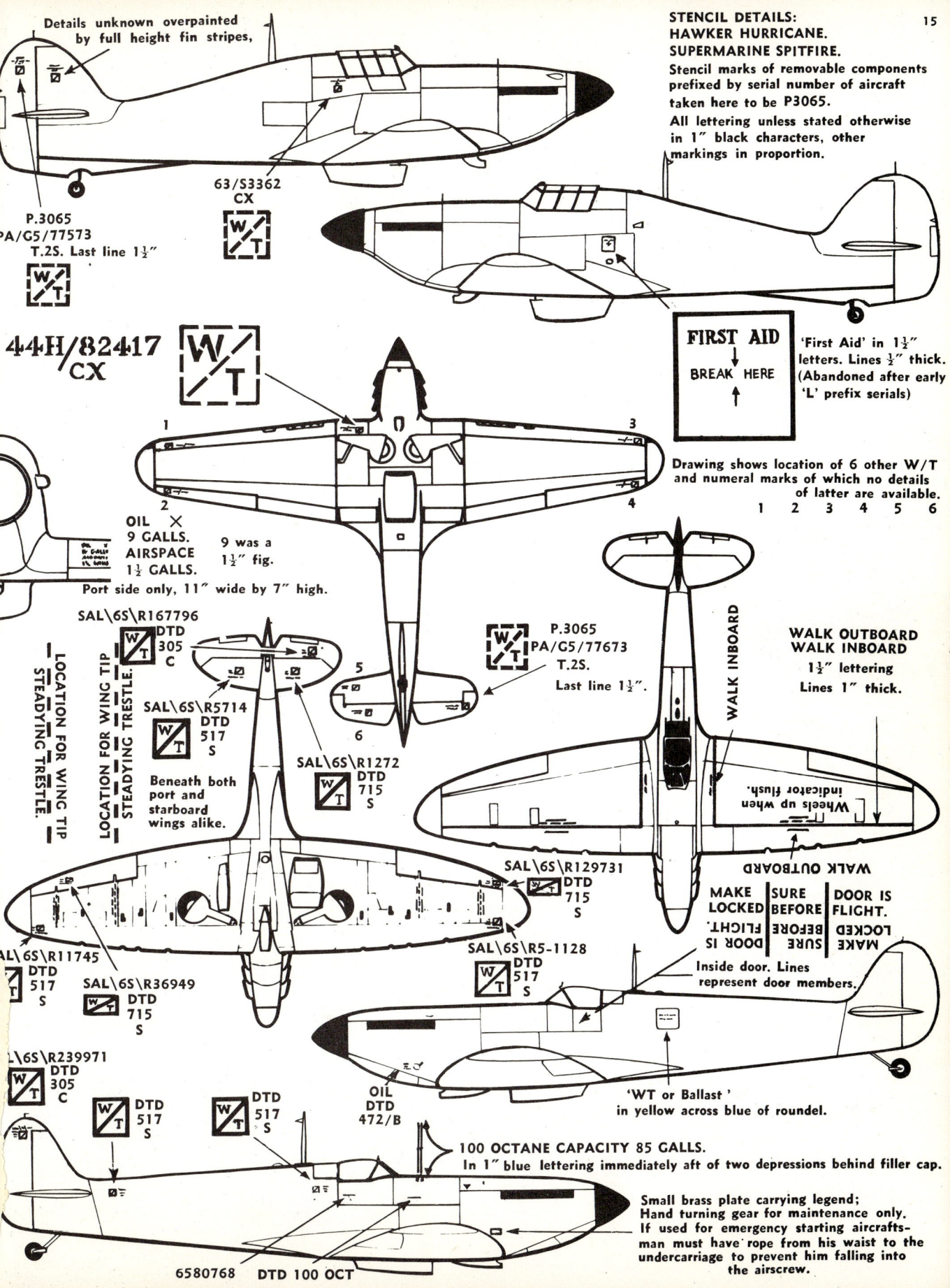

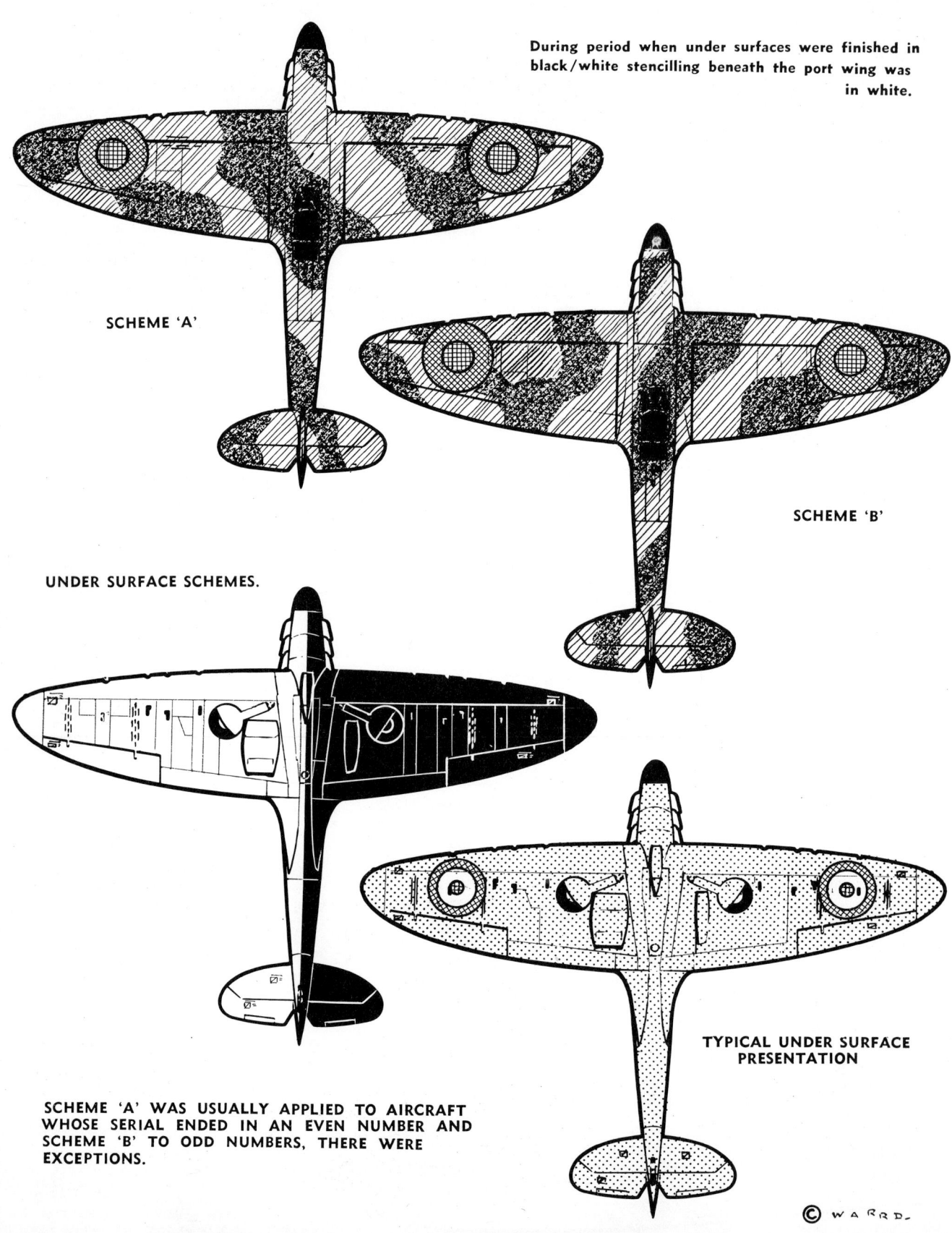

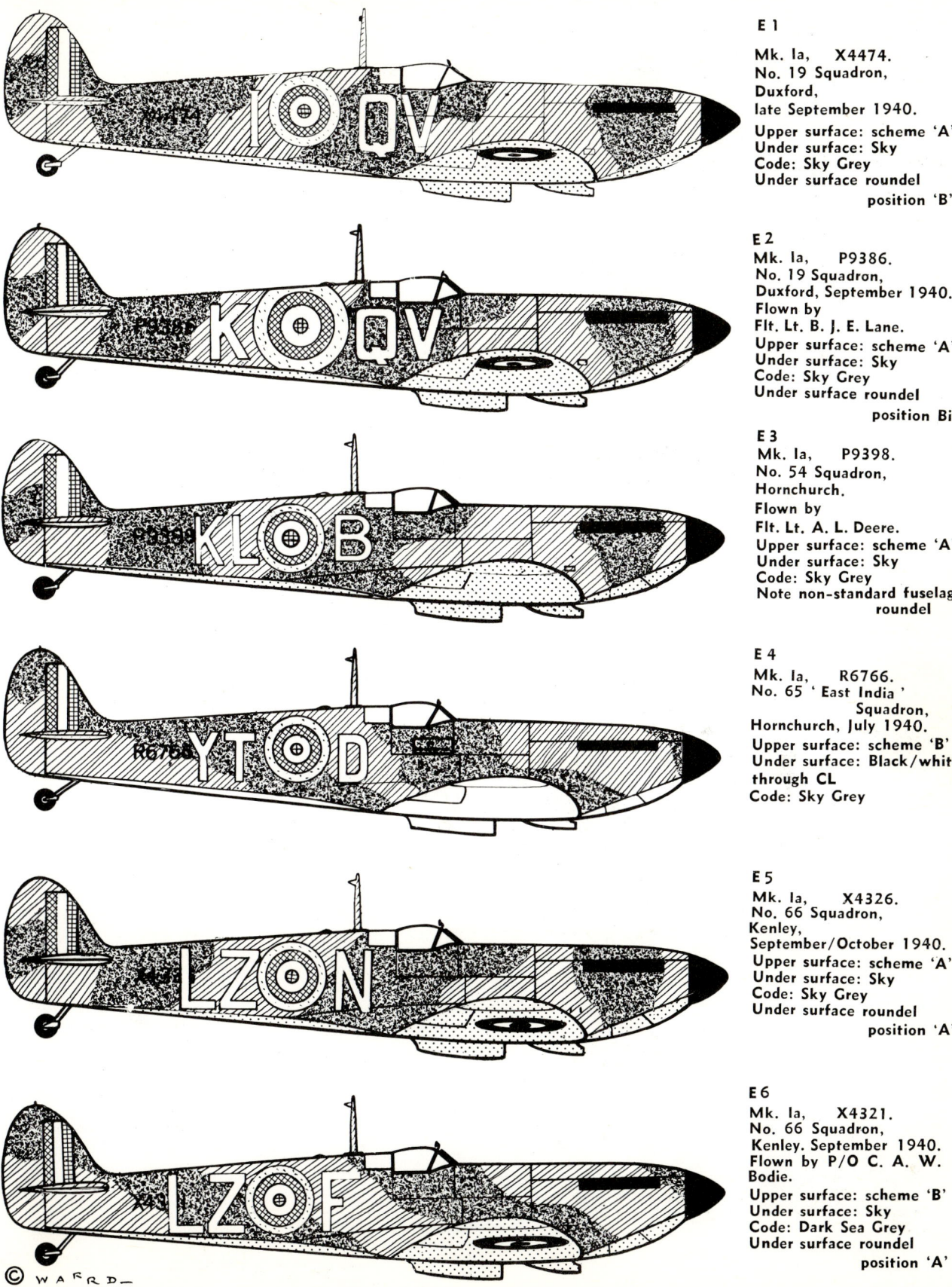

E 1
Mk. Ia, X4474.
No. 19 Squadron,
Duxford,
late September 1940.
Upper surface: scheme 'A'
Under surface: Sky
Code: Sky Grey
Under surface roundel
position 'B'

E 2
Mk. Ia, P9386.
No. 19 Squadron,
Duxford, September 1940.
Flown by
Flt. Lt. B. J. E. Lane.
Upper surface: scheme 'A'
Under surface: Sky
Code: Sky Grey
Under surface roundel
position Bi

E 3
Mk. Ia, P9398.
No. 54 Squadron,
Hornchurch.
Flown by
Flt. Lt. A. L. Deere.
Upper surface: scheme 'A'
Under surface: Sky
Code: Sky Grey
Note non-standard fuselage
roundel

E 4
Mk. Ia, R6766.
No. 65 'East India'
Squadron,
Hornchurch, July 1940.
Upper surface: scheme 'B'
Under surface: Black/white
through CL
Code: Sky Grey

E 5
Mk. Ia, X4326.
No. 66 Squadron,
Kenley,
September/October 1940.
Upper surface: scheme 'A'
Under surface: Sky
Code: Sky Grey
Under surface roundel
position 'A'

E 6
Mk. Ia, X4321.
No. 66 Squadron,
Kenley. September 1940.
Flown by P/O C. A. W.
Bodie.
Upper surface: scheme 'B'
Under surface: Sky
Code: Dark Sea Grey
Under surface roundel
position 'A'

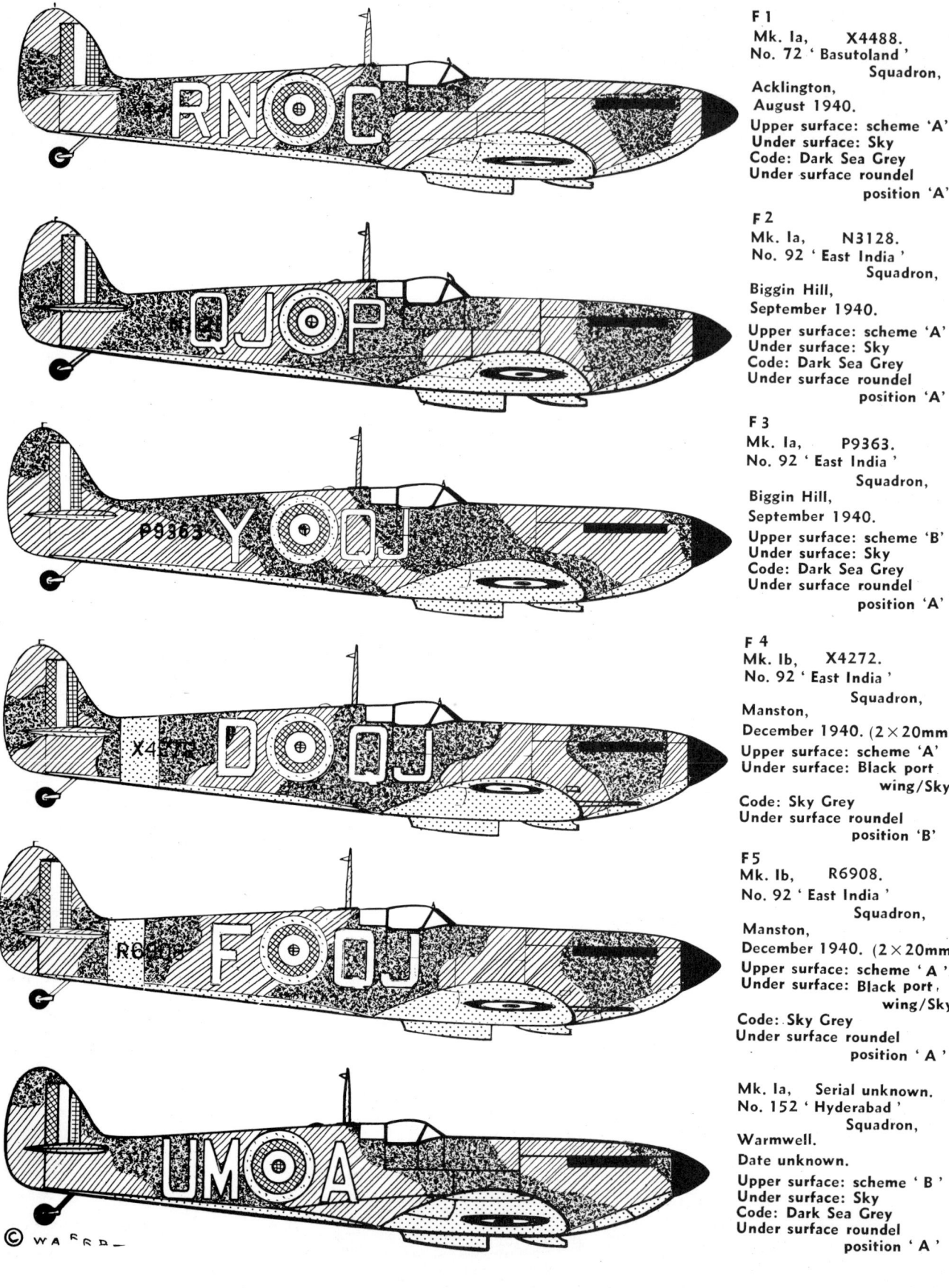

F 1
Mk. Ia, X4488.
No. 72 'Basutoland'
        Squadron,
Acklington,
August 1940.
Upper surface: scheme 'A'
Under surface: Sky
Code: Dark Sea Grey
Under surface roundel
        position 'A'

F 2
Mk. Ia, N3128.
No. 92 'East India'
        Squadron,
Biggin Hill,
September 1940.
Upper surface: scheme 'A'
Under surface: Sky
Code: Dark Sea Grey
Under surface roundel
        position 'A'

F 3
Mk. Ia, P9363.
No. 92 'East India'
        Squadron,
Biggin Hill,
September 1940.
Upper surface: scheme 'B'
Under surface: Sky
Code: Dark Sea Grey
Under surface roundel
        position 'A'

F 4
Mk. Ib, X4272.
No. 92 'East India'
        Squadron,
Manston,
December 1940. (2×20mm.)
Upper surface: scheme 'A'
Under surface: Black port
        wing/Sky
Code: Sky Grey
Under surface roundel
        position 'B'

F 5
Mk. Ib, R6908.
No. 92 'East India'
        Squadron,
Manston,
December 1940. (2×20mm.)
Upper surface: scheme 'A'
Under surface: Black port
        wing/Sky
Code: Sky Grey
Under surface roundel
        position 'A'

Mk. Ia, Serial unknown.
No. 152 'Hyderabad'
        Squadron,
Warmwell.
Date unknown.
Upper surface: scheme 'B'
Under surface: Sky
Code: Dark Sea Grey
Under surface roundel
        position 'A'

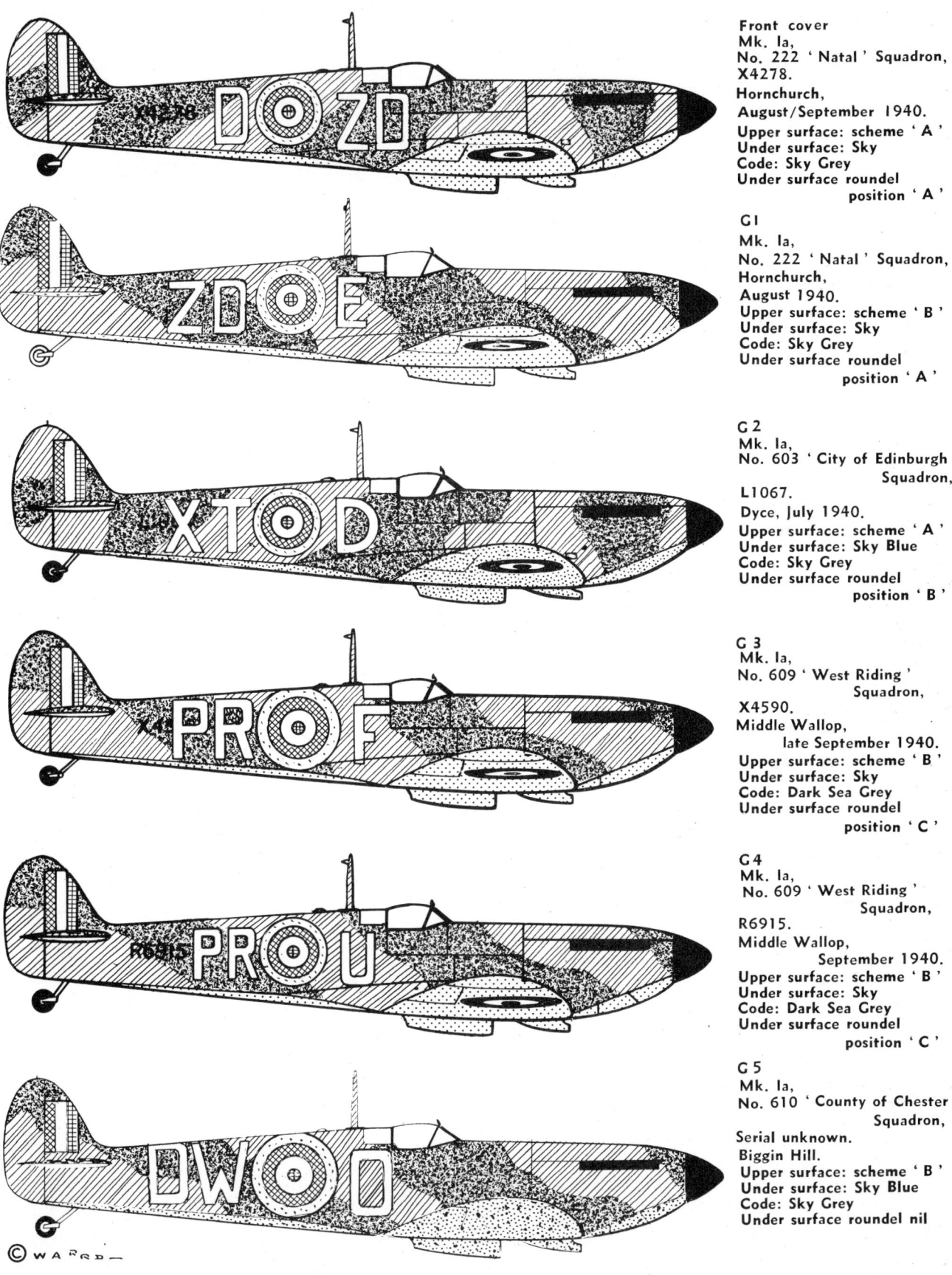

Front cover
Mk. Ia,
No. 222 'Natal' Squadron,
X4278.
Hornchurch,
August/September 1940.
Upper surface: scheme 'A'
Under surface: Sky
Code: Sky Grey
Under surface roundel position 'A'

G1
Mk. Ia,
No. 222 'Natal' Squadron,
Hornchurch,
August 1940.
Upper surface: scheme 'B'
Under surface: Sky
Code: Sky Grey
Under surface roundel position 'A'

G2
Mk. Ia,
No. 603 'City of Edinburgh' Squadron,
L1067.
Dyce, July 1940.
Upper surface: scheme 'A'
Under surface: Sky Blue
Code: Sky Grey
Under surface roundel position 'B'

G3
Mk. Ia,
No. 609 'West Riding' Squadron,
X4590.
Middle Wallop,
late September 1940.
Upper surface: scheme 'B'
Under surface: Sky
Code: Dark Sea Grey
Under surface roundel position 'C'

G4
Mk. Ia,
No. 609 'West Riding' Squadron,
R6915.
Middle Wallop,
September 1940.
Upper surface: scheme 'B'
Under surface: Sky
Code: Dark Sea Grey
Under surface roundel position 'C'

G5
Mk. Ia,
No. 610 'County of Chester' Squadron,
Serial unknown.
Biggin Hill.
Upper surface: scheme 'B'
Under surface: Sky Blue
Code: Sky Grey
Under surface roundel nil

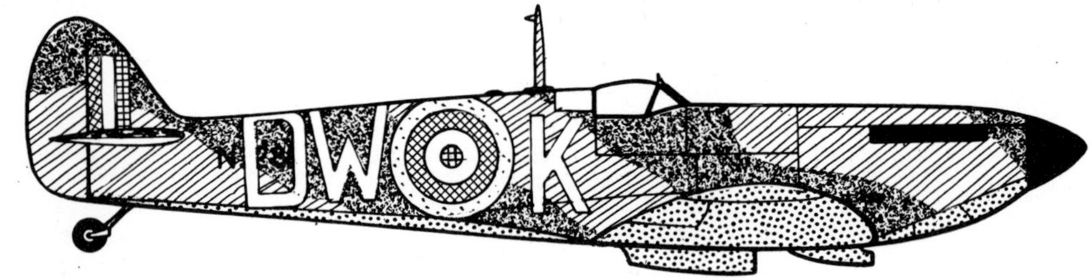

G 6
Mk. Ia,
No. 610 'County of Chester' Squadron,
N3289.
Biggin Hill.
Upper surface: scheme 'B'
Under surface: Sky Blue
Code: Sky Grey
Under surface roundel nil

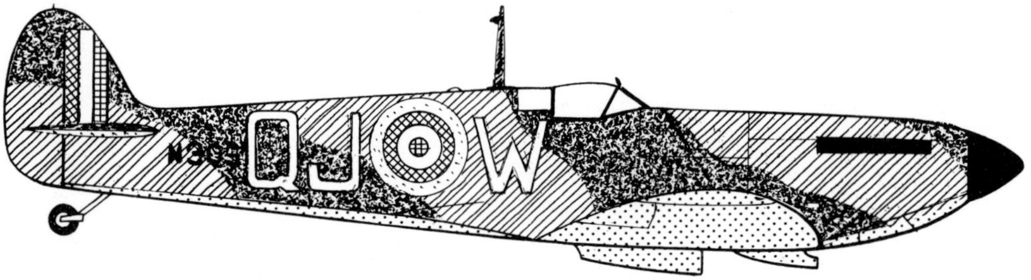

Title page
Mk. Ia,   N3093.
No. 616 'South Yorkshire' Squadron,
flown by
        Flt.-Lt. D. E. Gillam.
Upper surface: scheme 'B'
Sky under surfaces with
        black port wing
Under surface roundel nil

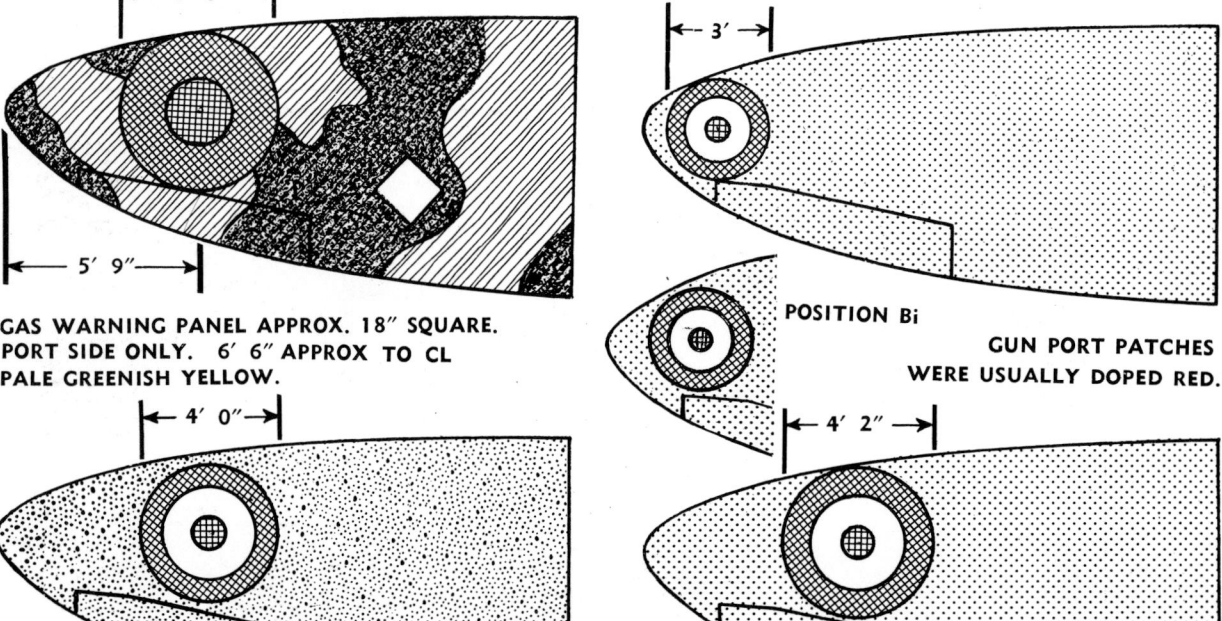

DARK GREEN | DARK EARTH | SKY | SKY BLUE | AZURE BLUE
RED | BLUE | WHITE | YELLOW | BLACK

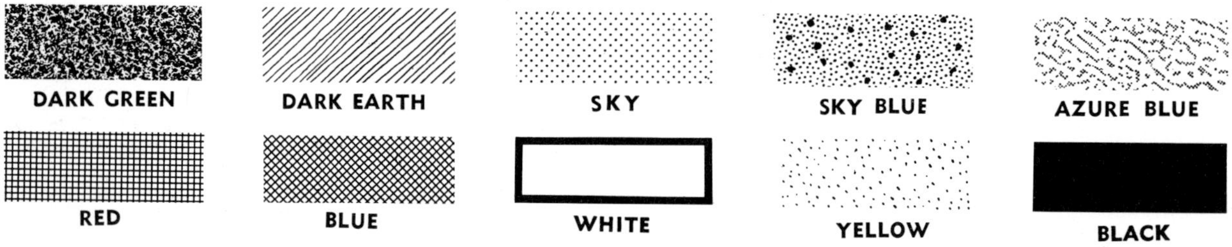

SPITFIRE ROUNDEL POSITIONS AND DIMENSIONS.

STANDARD POSITION OF UPPER SURFACE ROUNDEL.   UNDER SURFACE ROUNDEL POSITION 'B'

GAS WARNING PANEL APPROX. 18" SQUARE. PORT SIDE ONLY. 6' 6" APPROX TO CL PALE GREENISH YELLOW.

POSITION Bi

GUN PORT PATCHES WERE USUALLY DOPED RED.

UNDER SURFACE ROUNDEL POSITION 'A'   UNDER SURFACE ROUNDEL POSITION 'C'

THE MESSERSCHMITT BF 109E

The only single-engined, single-seat fighter used by the Luftwaffe during the Battle of Britain, the Messerschmitt Bf 109E, differed from its main opponents, the Spitfires and Hurricanes, in that it was a development of the basic design, revised and improved in the light of actual combat experience. Although designed around the same time as the two British aircraft, the Bf 109 had entered service more quickly and had gained combat experience in Spain before either of the former had even entered service. This was fortunate for the Germans as the initial models of the Bf 109, the B and C, had performances and armaments definitely inferior to the Hurricane, let alone the Spitfire, and had the Luftwaffe been forced to enter the war with the initial version of their aircraft as the R.A.F. had to, it is unlikely that the Bf 109 would have proved the equal of the French Morane 406, much less the Hurricane, Spitfire, Curtiss Hawk 75A or Dewoitine 520, and the whole war would probably have taken a different course. Such speculation aside, there is little doubt that in 1940 the Bf 109E was the most competent and combat-worthy fighter in service in Europe.

In July 1940 the Luftwaffe fighters were supremely confident. Many pilots had experience in Spain and Poland behind them, and most had flown during the invasions of France, Belgium and Holland. Their aircraft had a better service ceiling and dive performance than either of its opponents, and a far higher top speed than the Hurricane I. There has been much speculation as to whether the Bf 109E was faster than the Spitfire I or vice versa, but it seems that the balance depended on altitude; at 12,000 feet the Messerschmitt had the edge, clocking its best speed of 354 m.p.h. here, while the Spitfire performed best at 19,000 feet, reaching 355 m.p.h. at this level.

In armament, tactics, and general pilot experience, the Germans had a definite advantage, their mixed machine gun and cannon armament proving most effective in combat, and their widely-spread, pairs formations being far superior to the R.A.F.'s tight formations of three aircraft. Both British aircraft could out-manoeuvre the German, so that a capable Hurricane pilot who saw his opponent in time, could always hold his own. However, the Messerschmitt pilot could always break off combat by climbing, or pulling away from the Hurricane, or by rolling over and diving away from the Spitfire, a manoeuvre the latter was unable to follow The Germans did not regard the Hurricane very highly, and it was described by Gen. Adolf Galland as a 'Nice aircraft to shoot down'.

During July the German pilots felt they had gained air superiority over the Channel, but were surprised by the strength of the reaction when the attacks switched to mainland targets in August. When flying 'Free Chase' hunting sweeps ahead of the bombers, the Messerschmitts were in their element and were in a position to call the tune, giving the R.A.F. fighters a very bad time, inflicting heavy casualties. Later in the Battle, when they were forced to provide close escort to the bomber formations due to losses to the latter, they lost the initiative, and their short range reduced their time over target as a result of the fuel expended rendezvousing with their charges and staying with them during the approach to the target, and consequently their losses rose and morale dropped. During the fighter battles of October they were able to return to their favoured tactics, but by that time Fighter Command had learnt much, and this phase of the Battle petered out in a draw.

From August to October nearly the whole German fighter force was concentrated on airfields in Holland, Belgium and France, operating with Luftflotten 2 and 3, and the pilots of these units flew throughout the Battle without respite, becoming as exhausted as were the pilots of Fighter Command. Fighter units with the Bf 109E taking part in these operations from August included the Stab (H.Q. flight), I, II and III Gruppen of Jagdgeschwadern 2, 3, 26, 27, 51, 52 and 53, and Stab. and I Gruppe of JG 54. At the start of the Battle Luftflotte 5 in Norway included Stab., I and II Gruppen of JG 77, but these units were unable to take any worthwhile part in the fighting from this area, and I Gruppe joined the main force in Western Europe to take part in the later stages of the Battle, some elements of JG 1 also arriving around this time.

At the start of the Battle experiments with fighter-bombers were made by Eprobungsgruppe 210, which operated both Bf 109's and Bf 110's in this role during August and September. Further Bf 109E fighter-bomber units were formed, and although by October E.Gr. 210 become an all-Bf 110 unit, II Gruppe, followed by I Gruppe of Lehrgeschwader 2 had begun operations over England with the former aircraft. All the Jagdgeschwadern were ordered at this time to convert one Staffel each for the fighter-bomber role.

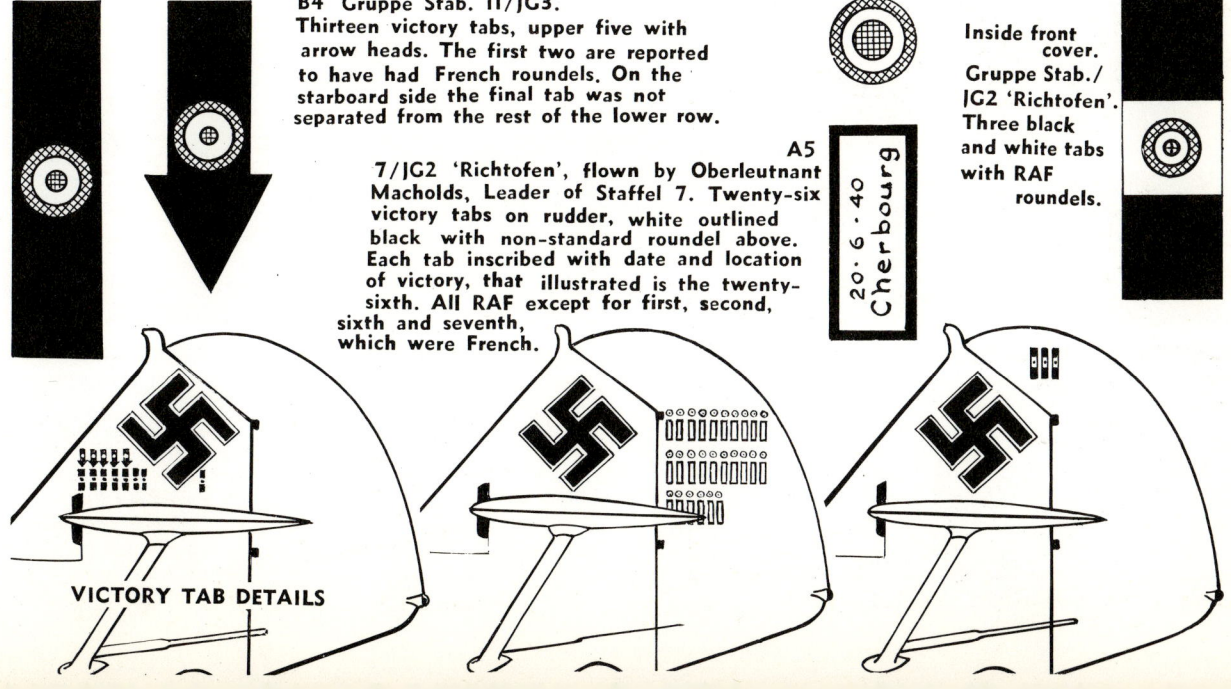

B4 Gruppe Stab. II/JG3.
Thirteen victory tabs, upper five with arrow heads. The first two are reported to have had French roundels. On the starboard side the final tab was not separated from the rest of the lower row.

A5
7/JG2 'Richtofen', flown by Oberleutnant Macholds, Leader of Staffel 7. Twenty-six victory tabs on rudder, white outlined black with non-standard roundel above. Each tab inscribed with date and location of victory, that illustrated is the twenty-sixth. All RAF except for first, second, sixth and seventh, which were French.

20.6.40 Cherbourg

Inside front cover. Gruppe Stab./JG2 'Richtofen'. Three black and white tabs with RAF roundels.

VICTORY TAB DETAILS

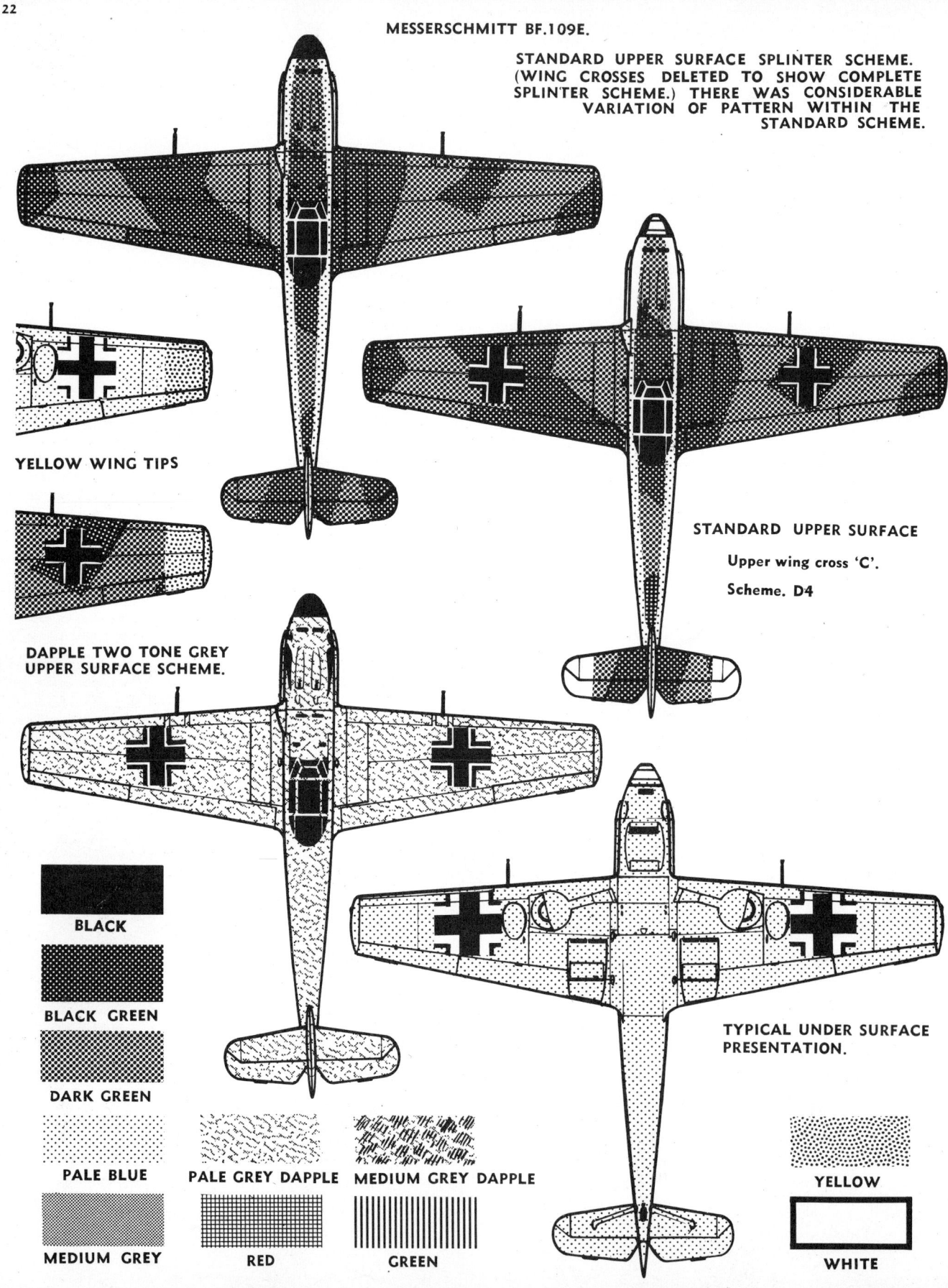

AIRCAM AVIATION SERIES
LUFTWAFFE
UNIT INSIGNIA

UI.S/No. 2

Circa Battle of Britain
July 1st – December 31st, 1940

JG1

JG2 "Richthofen"

JG2 "Richthofen"

Personal insignia Major Helmut Wick
"Horrido" (Tally-ho)

7/JG2 "Richthofen"

8/JG2 "Richthofen"

9/JG2 "Richthofen"

9/JG2 "Richthofen"

Personal insignia "Erika"

II/JG3 "Udet"

III/JG3 "Udet"

JG3 "Udet"

1/JG3 "Udet"

2/JG3 "Udet"

JG26 "Schlageter"

JG26 "Schlageter"

JG26 "Schlageter"

JG26 "Schlageter"

4/JG26 "Schlageter"

6/JG26 "Schlageter"

© WARD

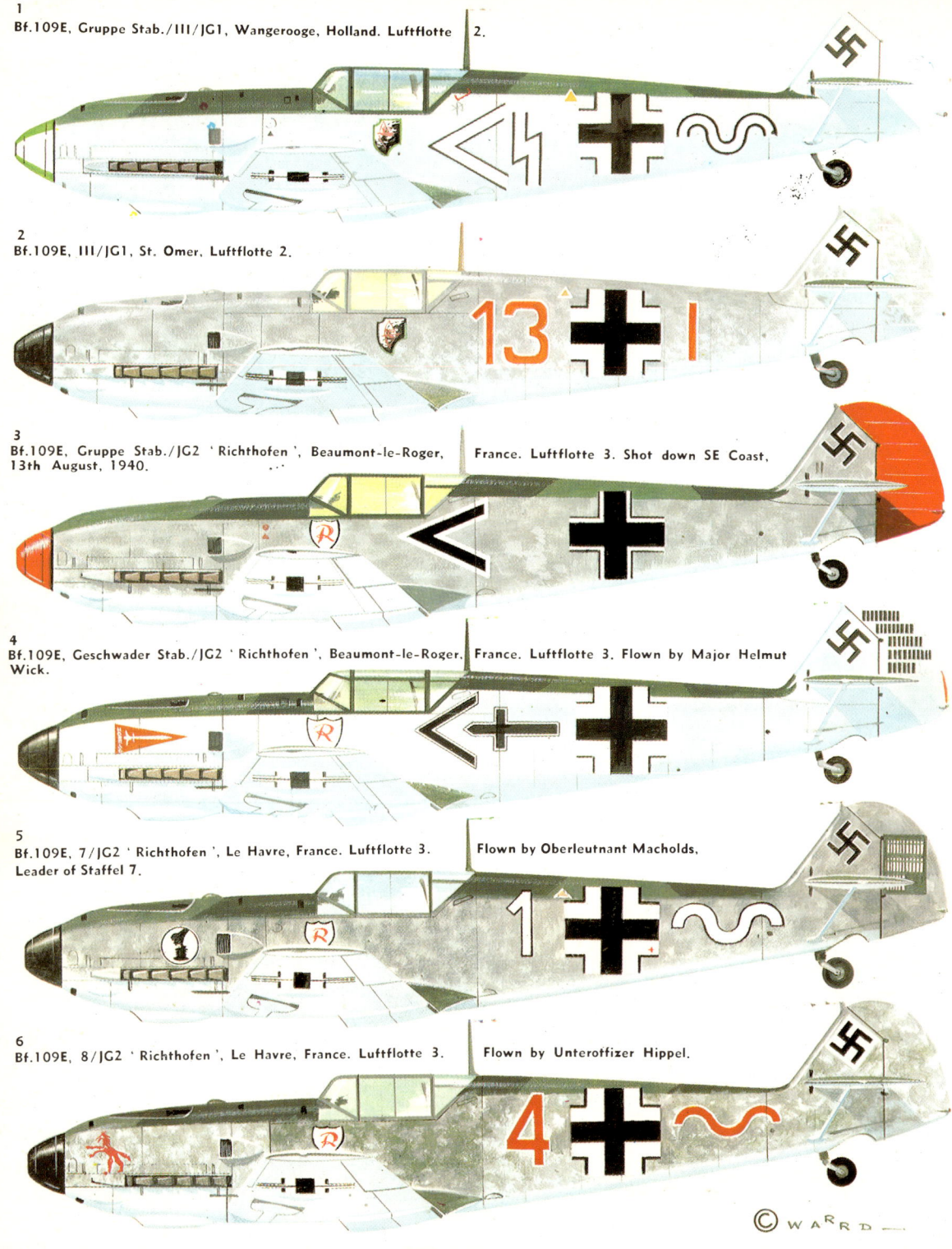

A

1
Bf.109E, Gruppe Stab./III/JG1, Wangerooge, Holland. Luftflotte 2.

2
Bf.109E, III/JG1, St. Omer, Luftflotte 2.

3
Bf.109E, Gruppe Stab./JG2 'Richthofen', Beaumont-le-Roger, France. Luftflotte 3. Shot down SE Coast, 13th August, 1940.

4
Bf.109E, Geschwader Stab./JG2 'Richthofen', Beaumont-le-Roger, France. Luftflotte 3. Flown by Major Helmut Wick.

5
Bf.109E, 7/JG2 'Richthofen', Le Havre, France. Luftflotte 3. Flown by Oberleutnant Macholds, Leader of Staffel 7.

6
Bf.109E, 8/JG2 'Richthofen', Le Havre, France. Luftflotte 3. Flown by Unteroffizer Hippel.

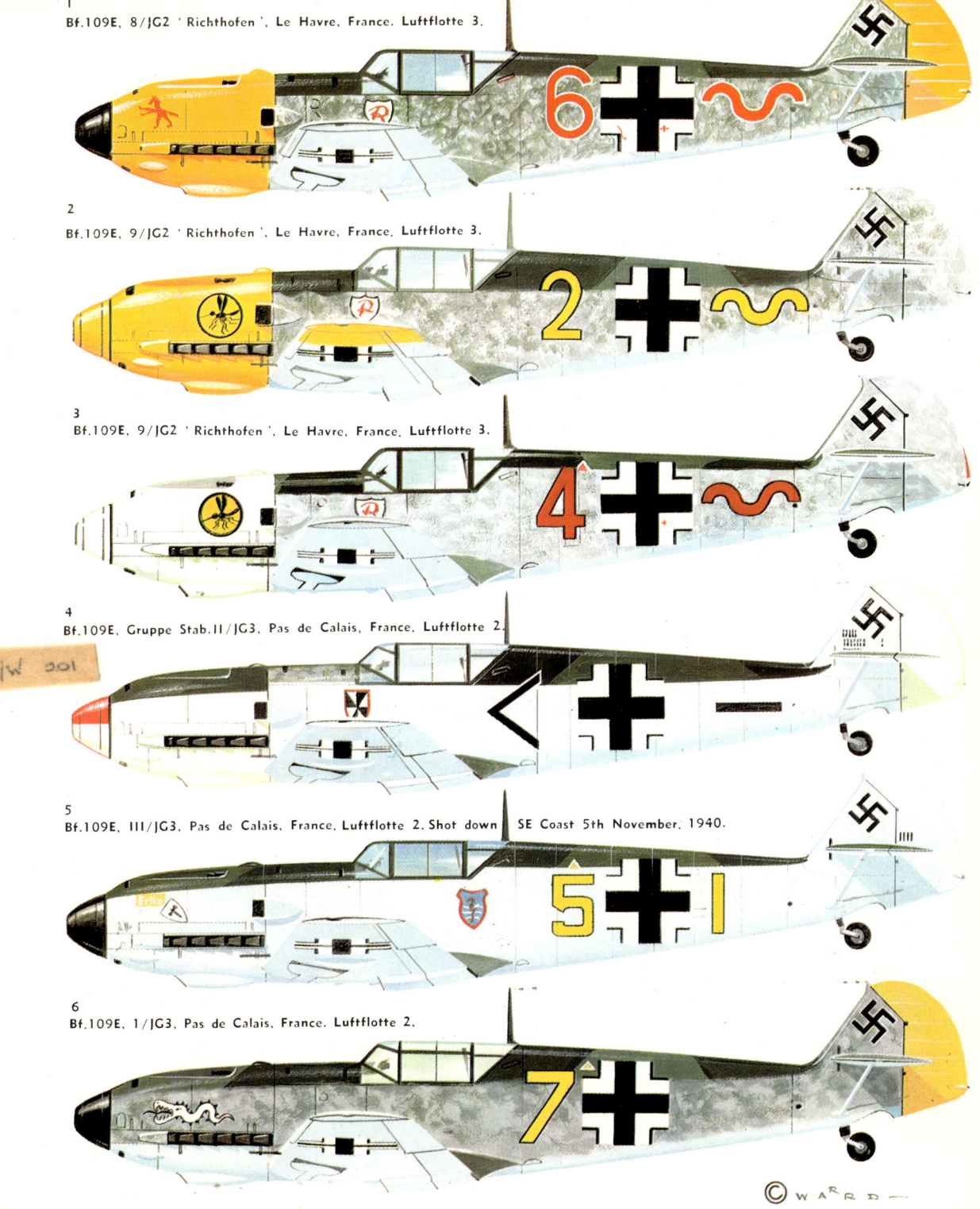

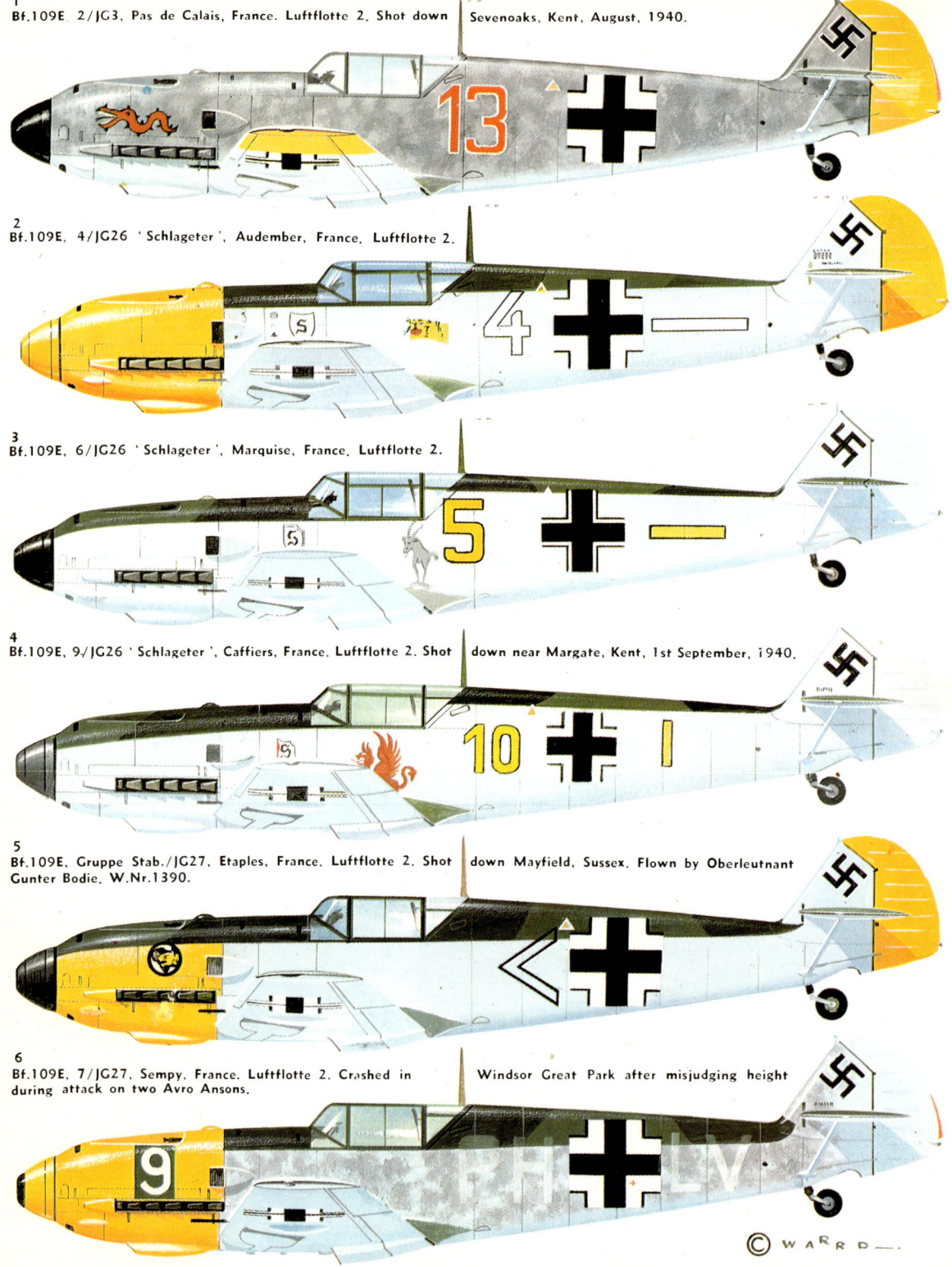

1
Bf.109E, 2/JG3, Pas de Calais, France. Luftflotte 2. Shot down Sevenoaks, Kent, August, 1940.

2
Bf.109E, 4/JG26 'Schlageter', Audember, France. Luftflotte 2.

3
Bf.109E, 6/JG26 'Schlageter', Marquise, France. Luftflotte 2.

4
Bf.109E, 9/JG26 'Schlageter', Caffiers, France. Luftflotte 2. Shot down near Margate, Kent, 1st September, 1940.

5
Bf.109E, Gruppe Stab./JG27, Etaples, France. Luftflotte 2. Shot down Mayfield, Sussex. Flown by Oberleutnant Gunter Bodie. W.Nr.1390.

6
Bf.109E, 7/JG27, Sempy, France. Luftflotte 2. Crashed in Windsor Great Park after misjudging height during attack on two Avro Ansons.

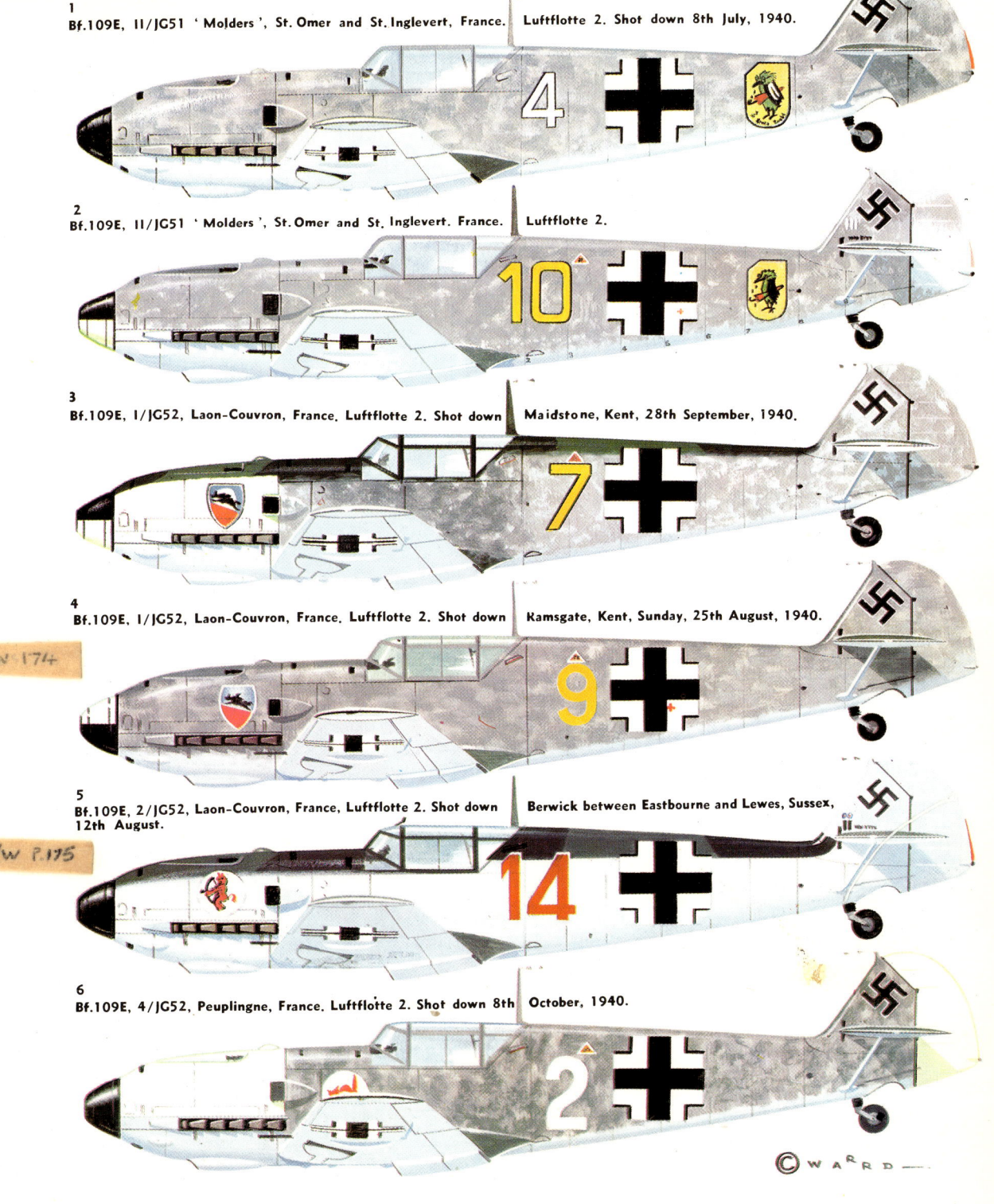

D

1 Bf.109E, II/JG51 'Molders', St. Omer and St. Inglevert, France. Luftflotte 2. Shot down 8th July, 1940.

2 Bf.109E, II/JG51 'Molders', St. Omer and St. Inglevert, France. Luftflotte 2.

3 Bf.109E, 1/JG52, Laon-Couvron, France. Luftflotte 2. Shot down Maidstone, Kent, 28th September, 1940.

4 Bf.109E, 1/JG52, Laon-Couvron, France. Luftflotte 2. Shot down Ramsgate, Kent, Sunday, 25th August, 1940.

5 Bf.109E, 2/JG52, Laon-Couvron, France. Luftflotte 2. Shot down Berwick between Eastbourne and Lewes, Sussex, 12th August.

6 Bf.109E, 4/JG52, Peuplingne, France. Luftflotte 2. Shot down 8th October, 1940.

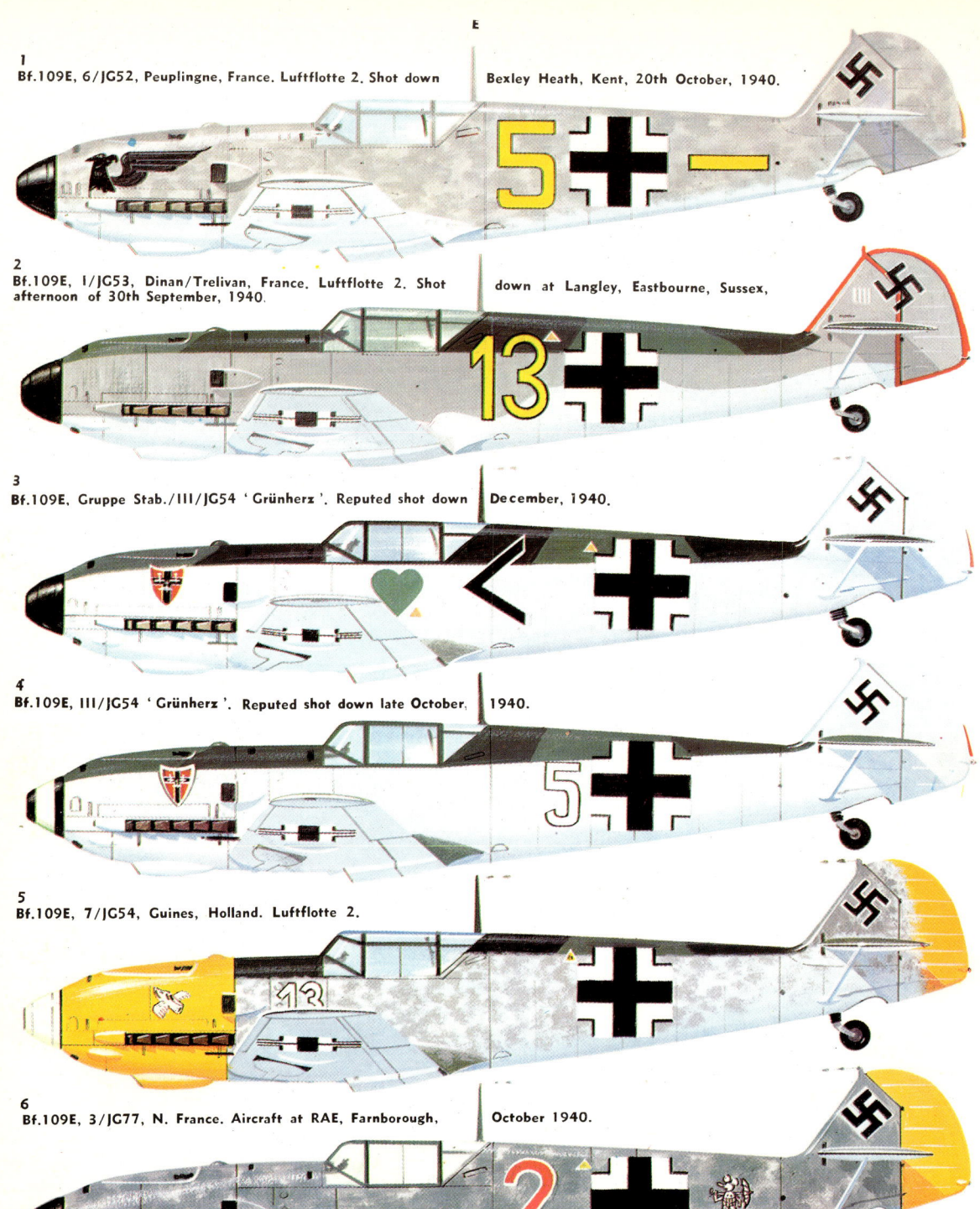

1
Bf.109E, 6/JG52, Peuplingne, France. Luftflotte 2. Shot down Bexley Heath, Kent, 20th October, 1940.

2
Bf.109E, 1/JG53, Dinan/Trelivan, France. Luftflotte 2. Shot down at Langley, Eastbourne, Sussex, afternoon of 30th September, 1940.

3
Bf.109E, Gruppe Stab./III/JG54 'Grünherz'. Reputed shot down December, 1940.

4
Bf.109E, III/JG54 'Grünherz'. Reputed shot down late October, 1940.

5
Bf.109E, 7/JG54, Guines, Holland. Luftflotte 2.

6
Bf.109E, 3/JG77, N. France. Aircraft at RAE, Farnborough, October 1940.

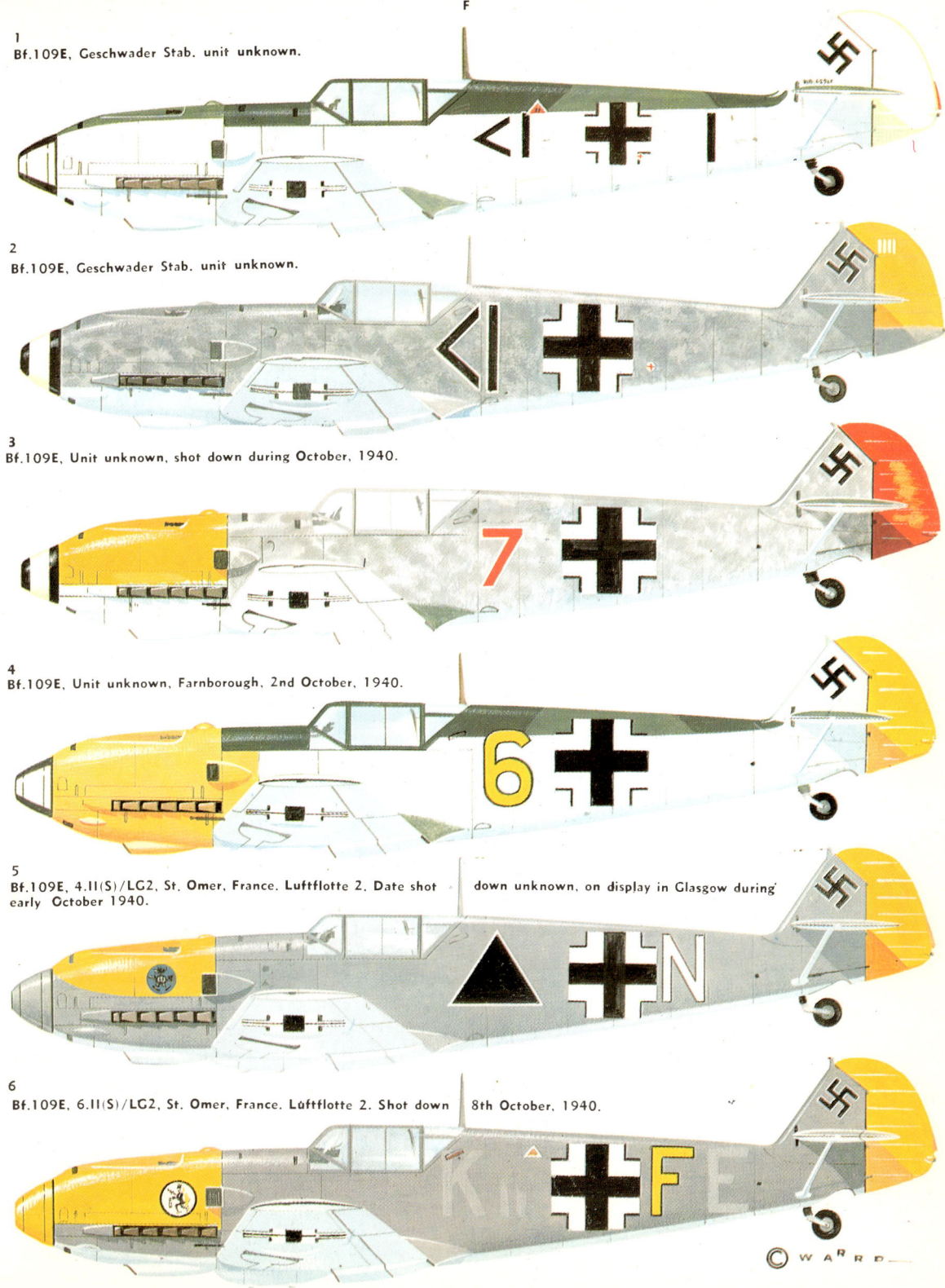

1 Bf.109E, Geschwader Stab. unit unknown.

2 Bf.109E, Geschwader Stab. unit unknown.

3 Bf.109E, Unit unknown, shot down during October, 1940.

4 Bf.109E, Unit unknown, Farnborough, 2nd October, 1940.

5 Bf.109E, 4.II(S)/LG2, St. Omer, France. Luftflotte 2. Date shot down unknown, on display in Glasgow during early October 1940.

6 Bf.109E, 6.II(S)/LG2, St. Omer, France. Luftflotte 2. Shot down 8th October, 1940.

AIRCAM AVIATION SERIES
LUFTWAFFE

UI.S/No. 3

UNIT INSIGNIA

Circa Battle of Britain
July 1st - December 31st, 1940

9/JG26 'Schlageter'

JG27

II/JG51 'Molders'

II/JG51 'Molders'

II/JG51 'Molders'

I/JG52

I/JG52

2/JG52

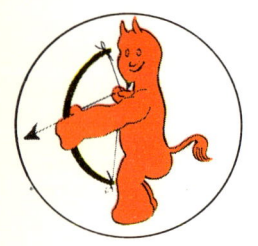
2/JG52

2/JG52

4/JG52

6/JG52

JG54 'Grünherz'

III/JG54 'Grünherz'

7/JG54

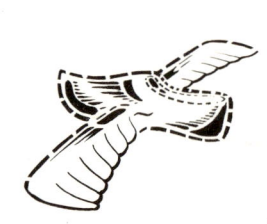
7/JG54

3/JG77

Personal insignia

4.II(S)/LG2

6.II(S)/LG2

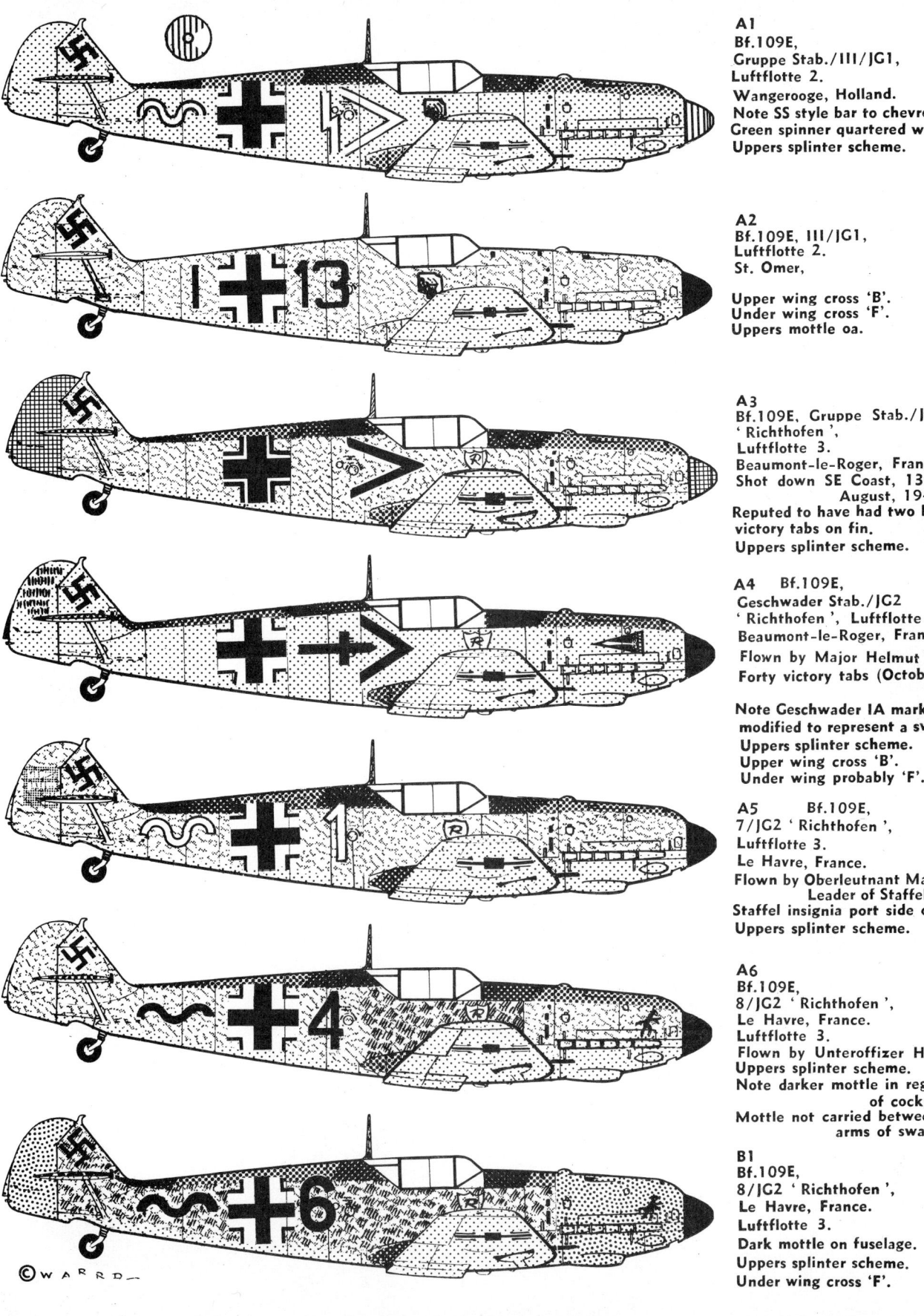

A1
Bf.109E,
Gruppe Stab./III/JG1,
Luftflotte 2.
Wangerooge, Holland.
Note SS style bar to chevron.
Green spinner quartered white.
Uppers splinter scheme.

A2
Bf.109E, III/JG1,
Luftflotte 2.
St. Omer,

Upper wing cross 'B'.
Under wing cross 'F'.
Uppers mottle oa.

A3
Bf.109E, Gruppe Stab./JG2
'Richthofen',
Luftflotte 3.
Beaumont-le-Roger, France.
Shot down SE Coast, 13th
August, 1940.
Reputed to have had two French
victory tabs on fin.
Uppers splinter scheme.

A4 Bf.109E,
Geschwader Stab./JG2
'Richthofen', Luftflotte 3.
Beaumont-le-Roger, France.
Flown by Major Helmut Wick.
Forty victory tabs (October) in
black.
Note Geschwader IA marking
modified to represent a sword.
Uppers splinter scheme.
Upper wing cross 'B'.
Under wing probably 'F'.

A5   Bf.109E,
7/JG2 'Richthofen',
Luftflotte 3.
Le Havre, France.
Flown by Oberleutnant Macholds,
Leader of Staffel 7.
Staffel insignia port side only.
Uppers splinter scheme.

A6
Bf.109E,
8/JG2 'Richthofen',
Le Havre, France.
Luftflotte 3.
Flown by Unteroffizer Hippel.
Uppers splinter scheme.
Note darker mottle in region
of cockpit.
Mottle not carried between
arms of swastika.

B1
Bf.109E,
8/JG2 'Richthofen',
Le Havre, France.
Luftflotte 3.
Dark mottle on fuselage.
Uppers splinter scheme.
Under wing cross 'F'.

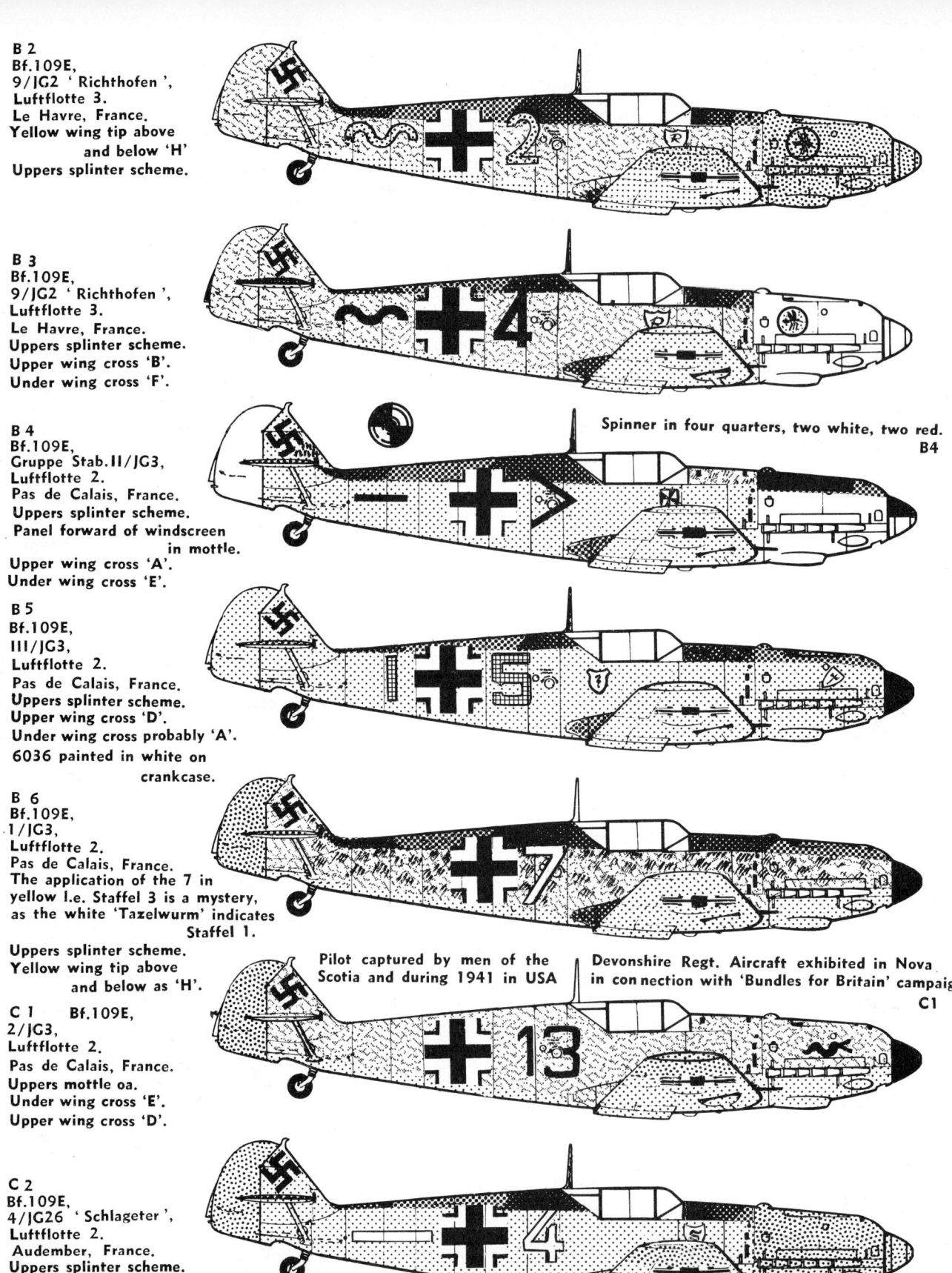

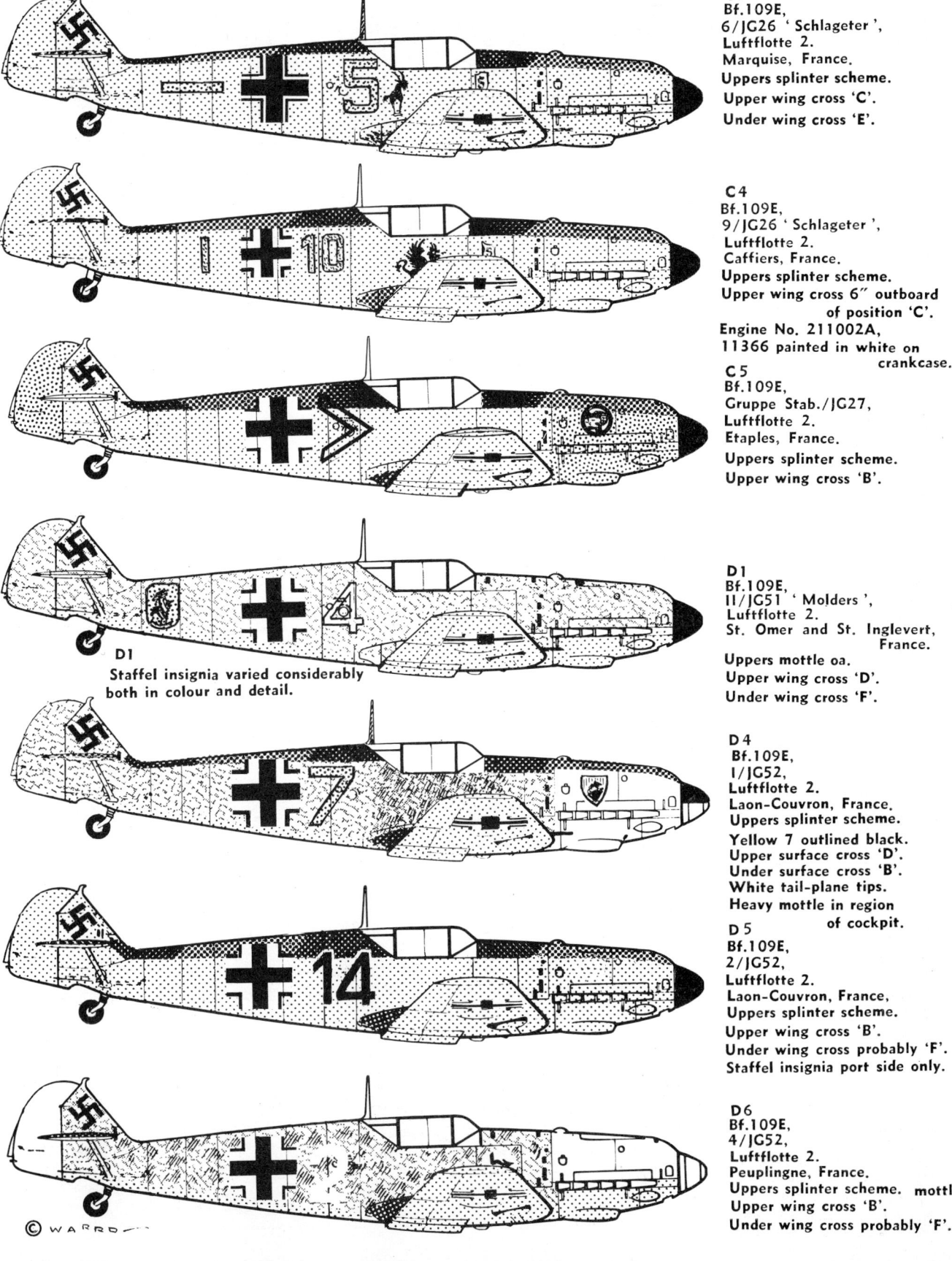

C3
Bf.109E,
6/JG26 'Schlageter',
Luftflotte 2.
Marquise, France.
Uppers splinter scheme.
Upper wing cross 'C'.
Under wing cross 'E'.

C4
Bf.109E,
9/JG26 'Schlageter',
Luftflotte 2.
Caffiers, France.
Uppers splinter scheme.
Upper wing cross 6" outboard
of position 'C'.
Engine No. 211002A,
11366 painted in white on
crankcase.

C5
Bf.109E,
Gruppe Stab./JG27,
Luftflotte 2.
Etaples, France.
Uppers splinter scheme.
Upper wing cross 'B'.

D1
Bf.109E,
II/JG51 'Molders',
Luftflotte 2.
St. Omer and St. Inglevert,
France.
Uppers mottle oa.
Upper wing cross 'D'.
Under wing cross 'F'.

D1
Staffel insignia varied considerably
both in colour and detail.

D4
Bf.109E,
I/JG52,
Luftflotte 2.
Laon-Couvron, France.
Uppers splinter scheme.
Yellow 7 outlined black.
Upper surface cross 'D'.
Under surface cross 'B'.
White tail-plane tips.
Heavy mottle in region
of cockpit.

D5
Bf.109E,
2/JG52,
Luftflotte 2.
Laon-Couvron, France,
Uppers splinter scheme.
Upper wing cross 'B'.
Under wing cross probably 'F'.
Staffel insignia port side only.

D6
Bf.109E,
4/JG52,
Luftflotte 2.
Peuplingne, France.
Uppers splinter scheme. mottle
Upper wing cross 'B'.
Under wing cross probably 'F'.

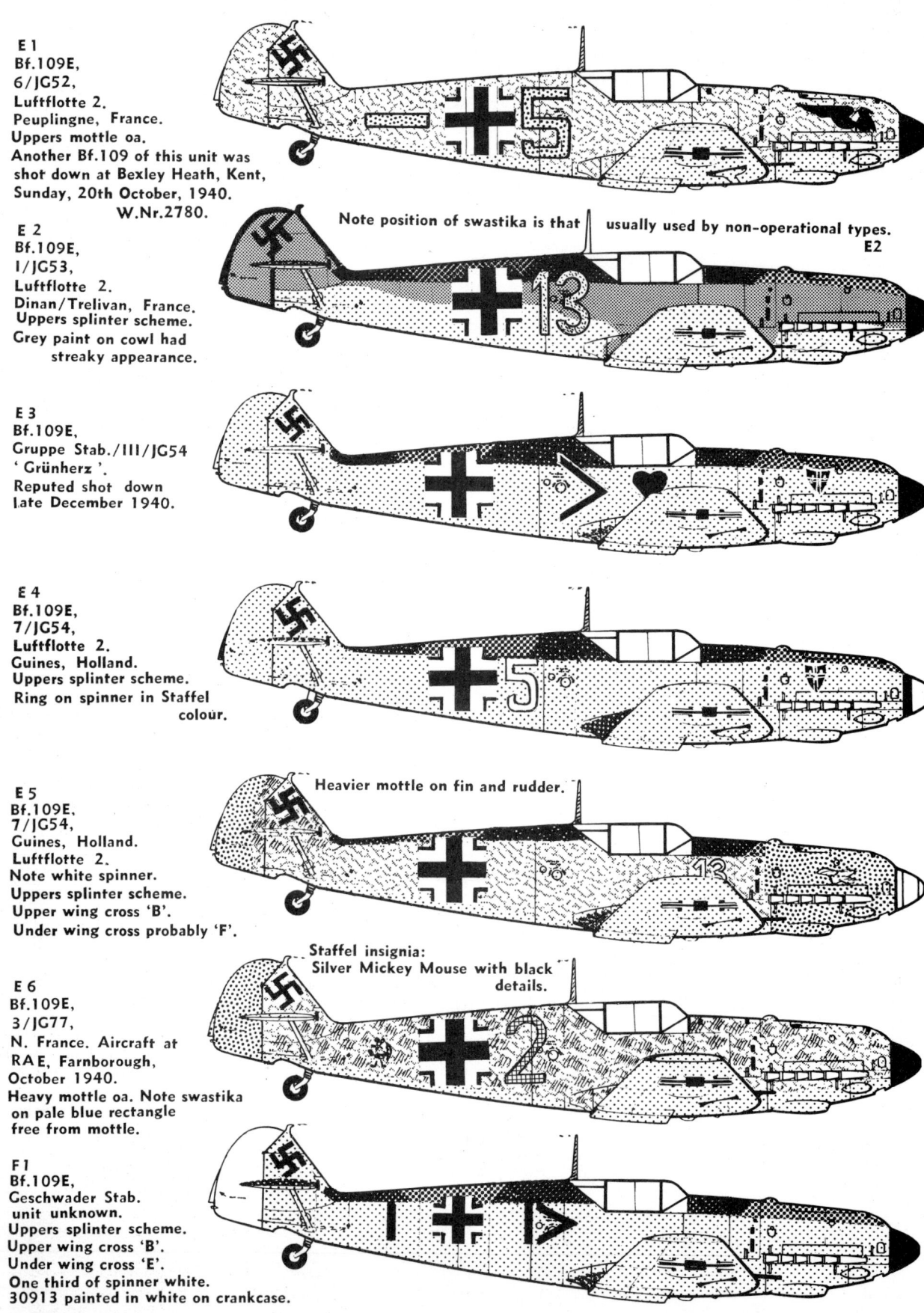

E 1
Bf.109E,
6/JG52,
Luftflotte 2.
Peuplingne, France.
Uppers mottle oa.
Another Bf.109 of this unit was
shot down at Bexley Heath, Kent,
Sunday, 20th October, 1940.
W.Nr.2780.

E 2
Bf.109E,
I/JG53,
Luftflotte 2.
Dinan/Trelivan, France.
Uppers splinter scheme.
Grey paint on cowl had
streaky appearance.

Note position of swastika is that usually used by non-operational types. E2

E 3
Bf.109E,
Gruppe Stab./III/JG54
'Grünherz'.
Reputed shot down
late December 1940.

E 4
Bf.109E,
7/JG54,
Luftflotte 2.
Guines, Holland.
Uppers splinter scheme.
Ring on spinner in Staffel
colour.

E 5
Bf.109E,
7/JG54,
Guines, Holland.
Luftflotte 2.
Note white spinner.
Uppers splinter scheme.
Upper wing cross 'B'.
Under wing cross probably 'F'.

Heavier mottle on fin and rudder.

E 6
Bf.109E,
3/JG77,
N. France. Aircraft at
RAE, Farnborough,
October 1940.
Heavy mottle oa. Note swastika
on pale blue rectangle
free from mottle.

Staffel insignia:
Silver Mickey Mouse with black
details.

F 1
Bf.109E,
Geschwader Stab.
unit unknown.
Uppers splinter scheme.
Upper wing cross 'B'.
Under wing cross 'E'.
One third of spinner white.
30913 painted in white on crankcase.

AIRCAM AVIATION SERIES

LUFTWAFFE UNIT INSIGNIA

U1/No. 4

Stuka Geschwader 77

Stuka Geschwader 77 Insignia

Stab Stuka Geschwader 77

Stab Stuka Geschwader 77

Gr. Stab I.St.G.77

Gr. Stab I.St.G.77

Gr. Stab II.St.G.77

Gr. Stab III.St.G.77

1./Stuka Geschwader 77

2/SC 77

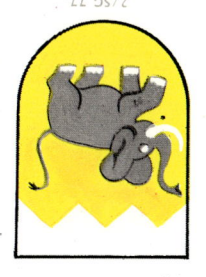
2/SC 77

3/SC 77

3/SC 77

4/SC 77

4/SC 77

5/SC 77

6/SC 77

7/SC 77

8/SC 77

9/SC 77

9/SC 77

AIRCAM AVIATION SERIES
LUFTWAFFE

UI/No. 15

UNIT INSIGNIA

Jagdgeschwader 1939–1945

Jagdgeschwader 'Schumacher'; Geschwader Stab/JG 1

JG 1 Pre-October 1943.

JG 1

I/JG 1

III/JG 1

JG 2 'Richthofen'

III/JG 2 'Richthofen'

1/JG 2 'Richthofen'

7/JG 2 'Richthofen'

8/JG 2 'Richthofen'

9/JG 2 'Richthofen'

9/JG 2 'Richthofen'

10 Jabo/JG 2 'Richthofen'

12/JG 2 'Richthofen'

JG 3 'Udet'

II/JG 3 'Udet'

III/JG 3 'Udet'

1/JG 3 'Udet'

2/JG 3 'Udet'

9/JG 3 'Udet'

Published by OSPREY PUBLICATIONS LTD., P.O. BOX 25, Oxford Road, Reading, Berks., England.

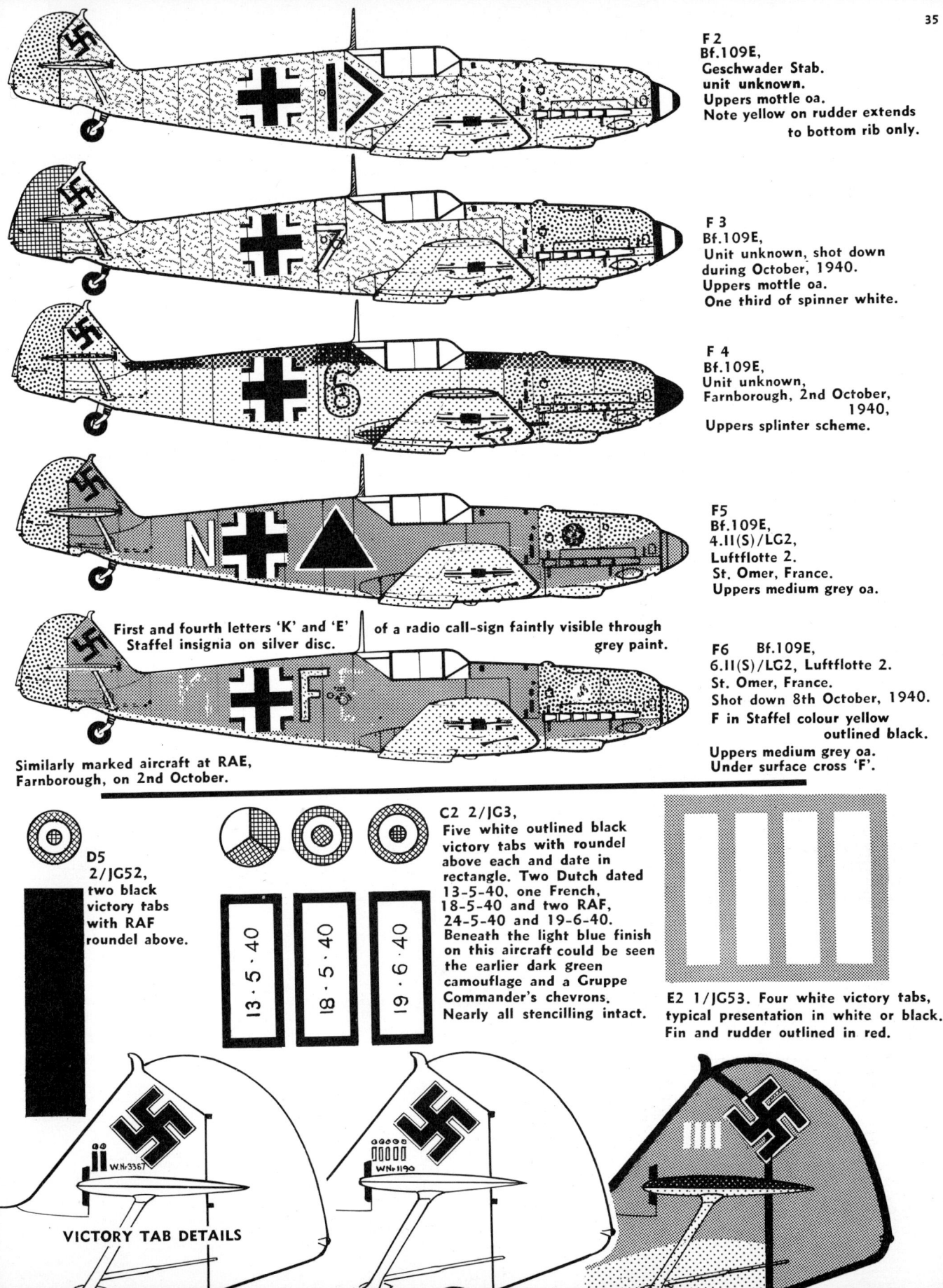

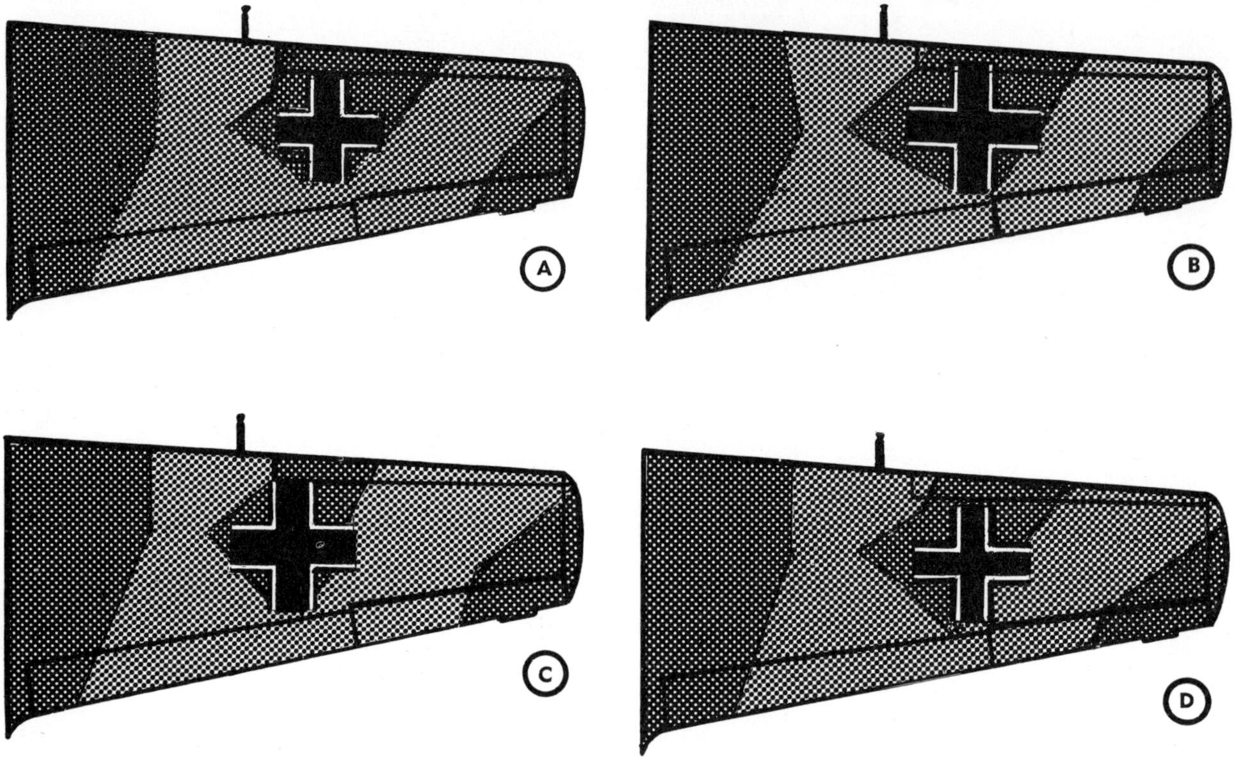

MESSERSCHMITT BF.109E

VARIATION IN UPPER SURFACE BALKENCREUZ

VARIATION IN UNDER SURFACE BALKENCREUZ

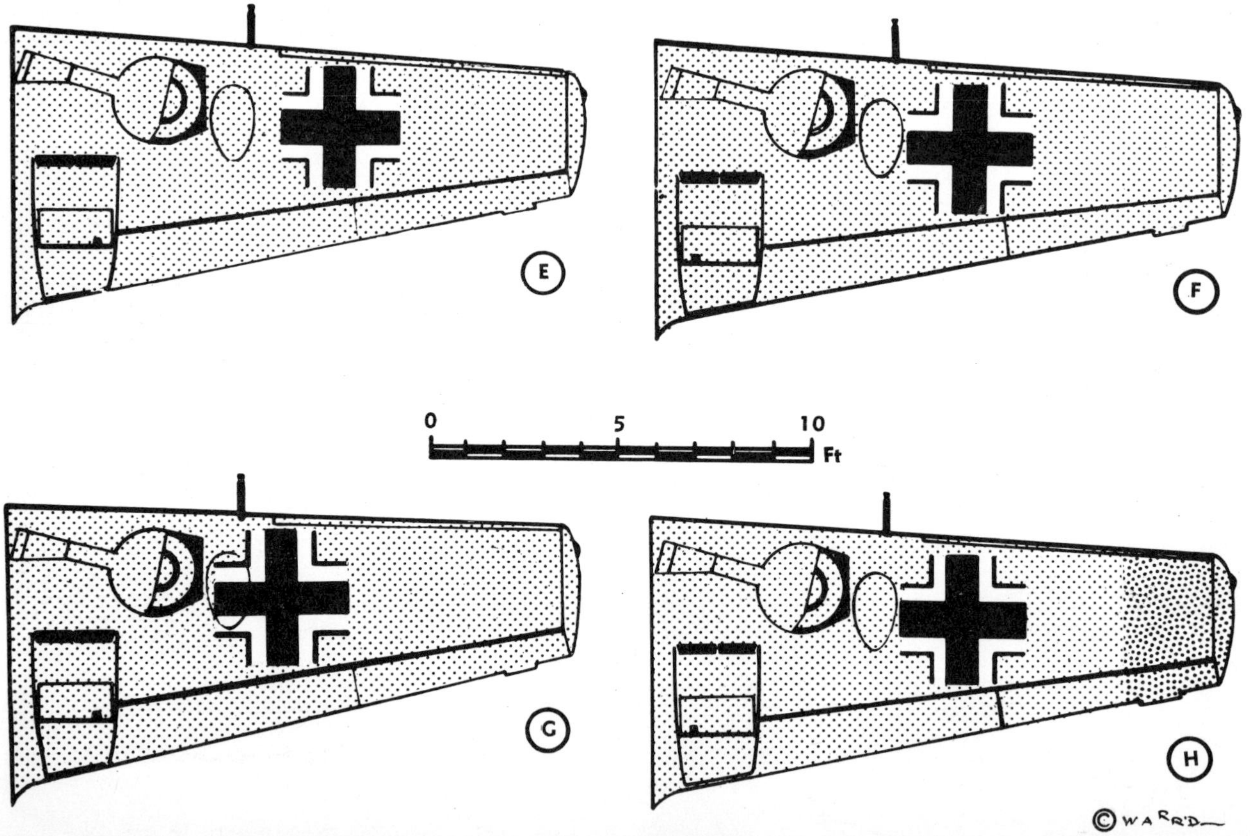

STENCIL DETAILS MESSERSCHMITT BF.109E

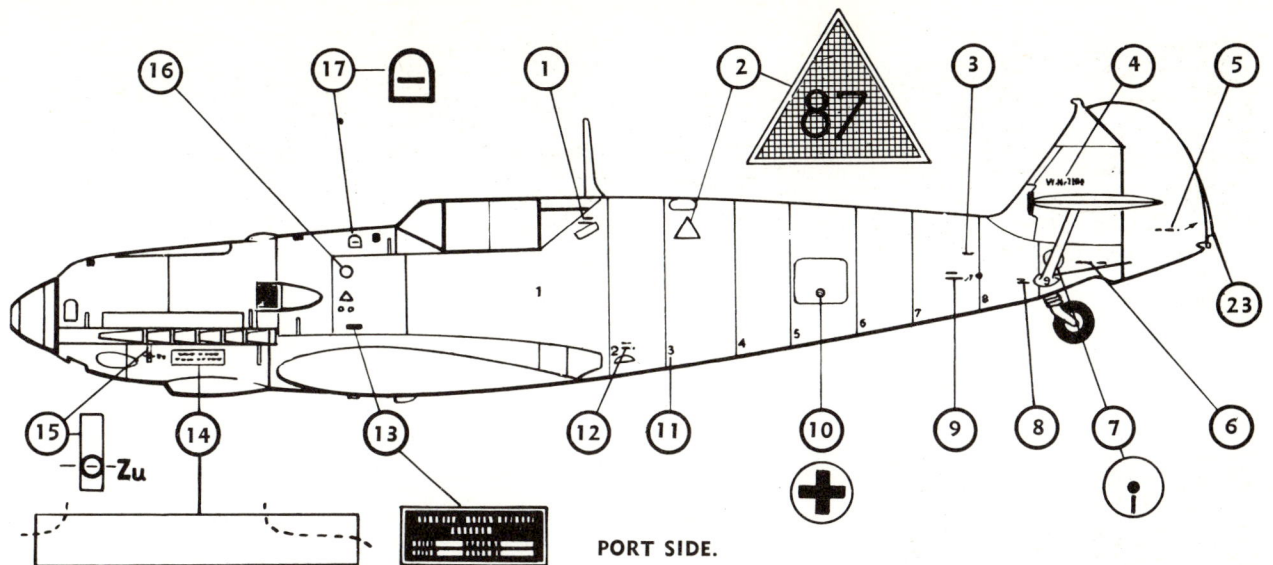

PORT SIDE.

1. Hier wingreifen. (In red, also red lower edge and side to aperture.) (Hold step here)
2. Red triangle with white edge. 87 in black. Triangle sides 20cm
3. WE
4. W.Nr.0000
5. Nicht anfassen. (With arrow at 45°) (Do not touch)
6. Reifendruck 4.5 (red) (Plug)
7. Circular access door with red locating arrow.
8. Hier aufbocken (red) (Jack here)
9. Hier anheben (with arrow 45°). These words were sometimes written as a single line, e.g. on upper edge of Gruppe bar on W.Nr.1480. W.Nr.1480
10. Red cross on an 8 cm white disc.
11. Numerals along lower fuselage, note raised position of 1 in line with rear hood frame.
12. Hier wingreifen. (In red, also red lower edge to foot hole.) (Hold/step here)
13. Manufacturer's plate (black and silver).
14. Vorsicht biem Offinen. Kühler ist im Houbenfetl eingebauf. (First sentence in red, second in black, the whole on a white rectangle 65 cm × 10 cm of which corners were often rounded off on re-sprayed machines as shown by broken line. (Beware intake (lit. opening)). Cooler positioned within.
15. Latch screw alignment mark in red, lettering black.
16. Circle occasionally in yellow and/or black rim.
17. Red outline and stroke.
18. Sauerstoff: Atemaerät. (Written in an arc above upper half of circular cover.) (Oxygen: breathing apparatus)
19. Vor Anschlup ab ölu Fett. (Grease point only)
20. Nicht betreten (Words and lines often in light blue on dark background) (Do not push here)
21. — Hier nicht schieben —
22. Frostschutzmittel (sometimes 'Frostschutzmittel Glykol'). (Anti-freeze)
23. Rudder trim tabs doped red, often sprayed over.

Airscrew specifications appeared on a white horizontal rectangular panel about 2 ft. 3 ins. from the blade tip.

NB. Although the lettering was invariably retained, these markings were sometimes reduced to just the outboard chord line running straight from wing leading-edge to flap hinge line. (20)

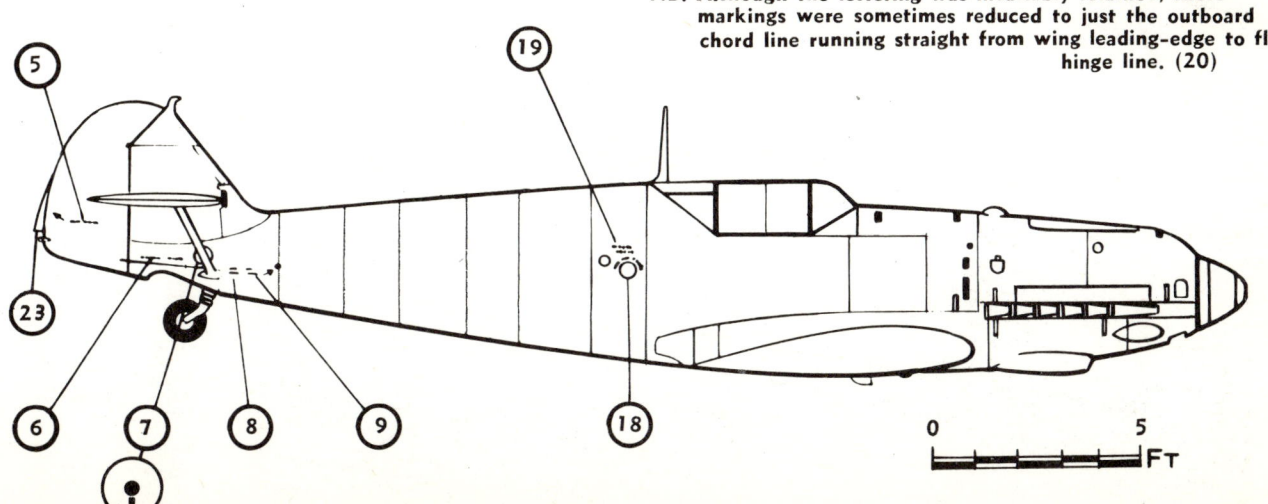

STENCIL DETAILS MESSERSCHMITT BF.109E

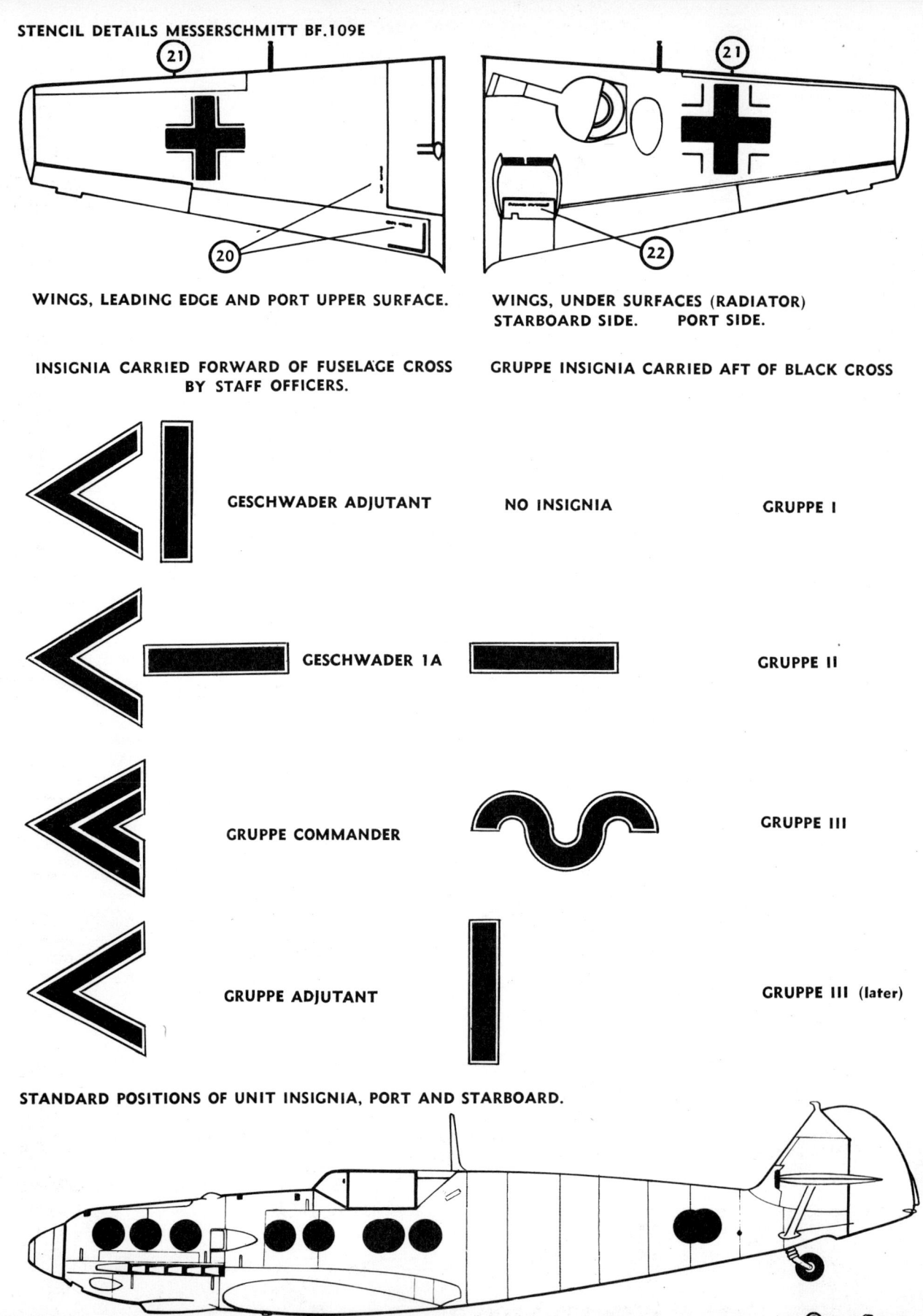

WINGS, LEADING EDGE AND PORT UPPER SURFACE.

WINGS, UNDER SURFACES (RADIATOR)
STARBOARD SIDE.   PORT SIDE.

INSIGNIA CARRIED FORWARD OF FUSELAGE CROSS BY STAFF OFFICERS.

GRUPPE INSIGNIA CARRIED AFT OF BLACK CROSS

GESCHWADER ADJUTANT	NO INSIGNIA	GRUPPE I
GESCHWADER 1A		GRUPPE II
GRUPPE COMMANDER		GRUPPE III
GRUPPE ADJUTANT		GRUPPE III (later)

STANDARD POSITIONS OF UNIT INSIGNIA, PORT AND STARBOARD.